GAME CHANGING COMMERCIAL CONVERSIONS

GAME CHANGING COMMERCIAL CONVERSIONS

Inspirational case studies of commercial property conversions

Game Changing Commercial Conversions

Inspirational case studies of commercial property conversions

First published in Great Britain in 2023

© Copyright 2023 Sustainomics Holdings Limited

Email: mark@sustainomics.co.uk

Web: www.sustainomics.co.uk

ISBN 978-1-3999-7493-6

A CIP catalogue record for this book is available from the British Library.

Cover design by Art by Avnie

Printed by Amazon.

DISCLAIMER

The information in this book does not constitute financial or other professional advice and is general in nature. It does not take into account your specific circumstances and should not be acted on without professional advice from fully qualified and independent advisors who should have a full understanding of your current situation, future goals and objectives.

Although the author has made every effort to ensure that the information in this book was correct at the time of printing, the author does not assume, and hereby disclaims any liability to any party for any loss, damage or disruption caused by errors or omissions, whether such errors or omissions result from negligence, accident or any other cause.

The author is <u>not</u> an Independent Financial Advisor, nor is he regulated in any way by the Financial Conduct Authority, and no inference should be taken in this book to suggest to the contrary.

DEDICATION

I would like to dedicate this book to my wife, Sharon, for her wonderful support, love, companionship and energy as well as to my four children: Ben, Jack, Katy and Emily who make me so proud.

They are my constant in life, my reason 'why' and who I firmly believe have the potential to make a positive change in the world and achieve great things.

I also dedicate this book to those that are prepared to create their 'North Star Vision', to believe in themselves, to step out of their comfort zone, to take action and to take control of their personal economy.

"It is not the critic who counts; not the man who points out how the strong man stumbles, or where the doer of deeds could have done them better. The credit belongs to the man who is actually in the arena, whose face is marred by dust and sweat and blood;

who strives valiantly; who errs, who comes short again and again, because there is no effort without error and shortcoming; but who does actually strive to do the deeds; who knows great enthusiasms, the great devotions; who spends himself in a worthy cause;

who at the best knows in the end the triumph of high achievement, and who at the worst, if he fails, at least fails while daring greatly, so that his place shall never be with those cold and timid souls who neither know victory nor defeat."

Theodore Roosevelt

TABLE OF CONTENTS

The Transformative Power of Commercial Property
Conversion – Mark Stokes   11

The Rock Factory – Michael Clay   17

From Strength to Strength – Kevin Edge   33

Unlocking Potential: A Journey to Commercial
conversions, Inspired by Personal Challenges
– Bjorn Harris   47

Transforming Buildings, Enhancing Lives
– Giles Harrison and Nana Banton   59

Enjoying the Development Ride
– Lucy and Stephanie Ingram   73

Transforming Spaces: The Journey of Victoria House
from Commercial to Residential
– Praveen Karadiguddi & Sumit Agarwal   87

My Journey to Creating Multigenerational Wealth
– Matt Kavanagh   95

Make opportunity count
– David Kemp and Michael McQuade   107

Transitioning from the world of corporate to property
development – Jay Lall   123

Dawson House – Michelle Lucas and Jo Balston   137

Turning a Victorian Pub into an energy efficient
co-living home – Cathy Mocke   149

The story of a 19th century Gentlemen's club restored
to its full glory – Richiko Olrichs   165

Scaling Up – Alex Potocki and Helen Clarke   177

Creating Value Through Structuring and Planning
– Tatiana Preobrazhenskaya   189

Oak House, the Project That Started My Commercial
Conversion Journey – Liam Ryan   203

Petals and Progress – The Floral Transformation in the
Heart of the Lake District – Jonathan Sharpe   213

My Humble Beginning... and the Journey Continues
– Lal de Silva   223

Look for opportunity where others aren't
– William Stokes   239

A journey begins – Jake Suthers   261

About Mark Stokes   273

THE TRANSFORMATIVE POWER OF COMMERCIAL PROPERTY CONVERSION – MARK STOKES

"Our built environment is the physical reflection of our collective dreams, aspirations and achievements" – Lucas Donovan

Book Chapter Authors

This book is dedicated to our amazing chapter authors who gave their time generously and shared their journey with humility and inspiration. My unreserved thanks and appreciation goes to each and every one of you who shared your successes and experiences for the benefit of others.

I am sure you will agree, after reading this book, that they have dared to achieve, had the courage to start, the tenacity to thrive and soared to success.

You are all amazing and will be a constant source of inspiration to many others in the future who would also like to take control of their lives and achieve their dreams whilst helping others.

Our wonderful chapter authors include:

Sumit Agarwal, Jo Balston, Nana Banton, Helen Clarke, Michael Clay, Kevin Edge, Bjorn Harris, Giles Harrison, Lucy Ingram, Stephanie Ingram, Matt Kavanagh, Praveen Karadiguddi, David Kemp, Jay Lall, Michelle Lucas, Mike McQuade, Cathy Mocke, Richiko Olrichs, Alex Potocki, Tatiana Preobrazhenskaya, Liam Ryan, Jonathan Sharpe, Lal de Silva, William Stokes, Jake Suthers.

Introduction

In the vast tapestry of real estate, there lies a distinct weave of projects that effortlessly marry past and present - commercial property conversions. These endeavours, while deeply rooted in brick and mortar, go beyond the physical realm. There are tales of rebirth—old structures regaining their charm, visionary developers realising their dreams, the repurposing of aging and redundant infrastructure and societies thriving through renewal and rejuvenation.

Imagine this - an old, forgotten factory, its once-robust walls now withering away. To the untrained eye, it's a symbol of decay, a remnant of a time long past. But to the discerning developer, it's a canvas, ripe with potential and possibilities. Through the lens of commercial property conversion, this dilapidated structure can metamorphose into modern lofts, trendy cafes, or even tech hubs that inspire the next big idea.

"Change is the heartbeat of growth" – Scottie Waves

Commercial property conversions encapsulate the spirit of change and innovation. As you delve deeper into this book, you'll uncover exemplary case studies that stand as monuments to this. Commercial conversion potential resides everywhere, ranging from forgotten warehouses resurrected as art galleries to old schools reborn as community centres, each endeavour embodies innovation, tenacity and the audacity to dream big.

It is much more than just that to the developers who are the catalyst of change. Without their passion, commitment and vision, none of this would be possible. As Steve Jobs said in his famous quote:

"Here's to the crazy ones. The misfits. The rebels. The troublemakers. The round pegs in the square holes. The ones who see things differently. They're not fond of rules. And they have no respect for the status quo. You can quote them, disagree with them, glorify or vilify them. About the only thing you can't do is ignore them. Because they change things. They push the human race forward. And while some may see them as the crazy ones, we see genius. Because the people who are crazy enough to think they can change the world, are the ones who do."

In the UK, of all the buildings that will exist by 2050 it is estimated that 80% already exist. It is clear that we will not be 'new building' our way into solving the current housing crisis. The opportunity to repurpose aging buildings, to meet the new requirements of the ever-changing demands of the population, are stark. Furthermore, this enables an incredible opportunity to support sustainable redevelopment and become a step closer to a net zero carbon economy.

To developers, these projects aren't just brick-and-mortar ventures. They are dreams carved into reality, opportunities to redefine skylines and leave a lasting legacy. It's a dance between preservation and innovation, with the reward being not just in the completion, but in the journey itself.

Yet, beyond the passion and the vision, there's a tangible financial lucrativeness of commercial property conversions which is life-changing. In a world where property price trends are ever-climbing, and land in prime locations is scarce, conversions offer a financially viable alternative. By rejuvenating existing structures, developers can unlock immense value, often at a fraction of the cost of new constructions and in a more sustainable manner. Moreover, these projects can qualify for tax incentives, grants, or special financing due to their sustainable nature and community benefits.

The margins in conversions, when done right, can be incredibly rewarding. Add to that the increasing demand for unique spaces in urban locales, and the financial prospects become even more enticing. For investors and developers alike, commercial property conversions can be goldmines of opportunity, offering returns that traditional developments often can't match.

Think what hundreds of thousands of pounds of profit would do for your family, your lives and how would it enable your vision? These results are there for everyone to achieve if they just make a considered start on the journey to becoming a commercial conversation specialist. Furthermore, a commercial conversion strategy also enables strong profits to be made, not at the expense of others but whilst enabling others.

We call this Creating Shared Value and potential is enormous to society. I see my mentees regularly creating homes for the homeless, shelter for those in distress, safe refuge for those recovering, sanctuary for those who have lived in fear and in all cases, the opportunity for all to start to live their best life.

The implications of these conversions stretch far beyond individual gains. They breathe life into communities. Old structures, once symbols of neglect, can spark urban regeneration, creating jobs, boosting local economies and fostering community cohesion.

"The best way to predict the future is to create it" – Abraham Lincoln

A rejuvenated building isn't just walls and roofs. It's a beacon of hope, a nucleus of community spirit. It's where children play, families grow, and elders reminisce. By repurposing existing edifices, we champion sustainable development, conserving history while curbing the environmental impact of new constructions.

Every beam restored, every wall repainted, and every space reimagined in a commercial property conversion resonates with stories from different eras. For a young couple, a revamped loft might be their first home. For an entrepreneur, a redesigned factory floor could be the incubator for world-changing ideas. For a community, a revitalised building is a symbol of progress and prosperity.

Places have the power to shape life's narratives and each of the inspirational chapter that follows will delve deeper into the intricacies of these transformations—the challenges encountered, solutions crafted and victories celebrated. It's a testament to human perseverance, vision, and the endless quest for beauty, utility and reaching one's dreams.

As you immerse yourself in these tales of architectural alchemy, let them inspire you. Whether you're a developer, investor, urban planner, or just someone with a penchant for stories of rebirth, there's a lesson, a message, and a spark awaiting you.

Let's embark on this journey together in the pages ahead, delving into tales of transformation, financial triumphs, and societal advancements. Witness the magic when vision, passion, and pragmatism converge in the realm of commercial property conversions. Here's to the past's charm, the present's dynamism, and the future's boundless potential.

THE ROCK FACTORY
– MICHAEL CLAY

With help from Business Partners Marc Turnier and
Andy Graham

"Have courage and be kind" - Cinderella

The Rock Factory

It started on a beach in Ibiza.

We were away on our two-week family holiday and having a great time with our young children, but also very conscious that these two weeks were just about the only time I was seeing the children. I was missing them growing up and outside of these two weeks, the rest of my life was consumed with work.

I used to work for a large consultancy firm which I loved - lots of international travel to great clients doing really interesting work, helping them transform struggling or failing parts of their businesses. However, getting on a plane on Sunday and coming back on the following Friday meant I had very little time with my wife and children, no time for fitness or personal development, and this lack of balance was really hurting me and all the family.

One of my friends had recommended the book 'Rich Dad, Poor Dad' and like many in the property world it was like a lightbulb going off in my head - I realised I had been doing everything the wrong way around. My life was paid for by work, but I had no time, I had limited assets and if work stopped, the money would stop!

From that point we set out to build a property investment business based upon our four principles:

- Balance (Between Work, Family and Fitness)

- Intergenerational wealth (passing wealth down three generations)

- Travel

- Charity

We originally invested in Student HMOs as a high cash flowing asset class. Building up a portfolio of Student HMOs allowed me to leave work two years later.

During those two years I became good friends with Marc Turnier and Andy Graham, both of whom were experienced property developers. In 2021 we collectively founded ArcVelop Investor Group to focus on commercial conversions as a way to build wealth through assets that would ultimately be less time consuming to manage than individual BTL or student properties.

'The Rock Factory'

The Rock Factory was a 3000sqft mixed use building in Kent. The large ground floor commercial space was originally used as a sweet factory used to make sticks of rock, whilst the uppers had been retained as two oversized and low-quality flats.

This building was on the open market, and we got in to view a little early due to having already curated a good relationship with the estate agents. We put in a slightly low offer but also went out of our way to meet the vendors and build a direct relationship with the agents' involvement - this relationship paid dividends later down the line.

After some brief negotiations that eventually went to 'best and finals', we had an offer accepted at £380,000 and the property was taken off the market. However, there was another interested party who were very upset that they hadn't been able to secure the property themselves. When the agent said that the property was sold, the disgruntled party went back to the vendors directly and submitted a substantially higher offer of £405,000 plus an offer to pay for the vendor's stamp duty and all fees. We calculated that their offer equated to about £425k, but was also proposing tax fraud as they were offering a total consideration of £425k but stamp duty would only be calculated at £405k.

We counter-offered at £405k but said that we wouldn't be willing to commit fraud to match the offer to pay stamp duty and asked the agent to do two specific things:

- Caution the vendor about accepting an offer from someone who was willing to commit fraud

- Highlight that an individual who was willing to commit fraud would also be willing to put in a high offer then get a valuation that shows the property has issues (which it did) and then late in the process go back to negotiate the price down

We were nervous about sticking to the £405,000 price, especially as our numbers worked at £425,000, but hoped our relationship with the vendor and agent would seal the deal for us. Very happily, the vendor accepted our revised offer!

Our plan for the project had three approaches:

- Fall back position – five flats. convert the downstairs rock factory to three flats under permitted development. Our numbers worked on this case but it was by no means our preferred option

- Seven Flats – Full planning application. Remove the roof and raise the height of the building to match the neighbouring building height to put two flats in the roof.

- Eight Flats – Full planning. Demolish part of the rear wall to create outdoor amenity space, reconfigure the internal floorplan and window placement more significantly, as well as raising the roof to add 2,000sqft to the gross internal area

We put in planning permission for the eight flat scheme shortly after our offer was accepted, with the view to get planning between exchange and completion which would significantly de-risk the scheme for us.

As we expected, the planning application was called into committee. If you ever get called into committee, I highly recommend that you go as it seemed to be so easy to make a good impression. We went to the full committee meeting well prepared, and we also saw plenty of other applications. We were the only property owners that turned up though! The simple things that we did that no one else did that day:

- Have a great scheme sympathetic to the area that will improve the neighbourhood and provide great places to live

- Turn up – I still cannot believe we were the only people who turned up to answer questions to try and help their planning application through

- Have really good 3D visuals showing what the building will look like after development. We even had close up detail of a flint wall that we would restore as this was highlighted as an important point by our heritage consultant

- Be prepared with a speech. We had a planning consultant write our three-minute speech to the committee about why they should approve the scheme. I practiced, practiced and practiced so it could be delivered in the timeframe

We got so many positive comments from the planning committee about how great the scheme looked, thanking us for attending and thanking us for being so prepared. The planning was passed by eight members to two - success! We obtained planning permission to convert the building to eight flats the day before we completed on the purchase!

Acquiring this property, situated within a conservation area, presented an interesting mix of challenges and opportunities.

The primary considerations revolved around issues of overlooking, the lack of parking in a densely built area, the need to create outdoor amenity space and a substantial amount of construction work to create the newly designed floor levels and plans.

Prior to the building work starting, we put a lot of time and effort into ensuring that we had a very comprehensive tender pack for the builder to quote against, including full drawings, structural engineers reports, a schedule for all fixtures and fittings as well as kitchen design and specs. We wanted to make sure that the prices we obtained were as close as possible to the final costs, and we were successful in doing this. We also wanted to ensure we could control and manage any variations to the work if they were required or advised by our contractors, building control or other interested parties during the development process.

We eventually selected a builder that Andy and Marc had already worked with on a previous and similar conversion.

This development took 10 months but it wasn't without its challenges - the biggest of which was an issue with the scaffolding. For example, the scaffolding contractor didn't put up the scaffolding according to the approved scaffolding design and a local neighbour just happened to be a scaffolding contractor and reported us to the HSE. This stopped work on site for six weeks and we had to take the scaffolding down and rebuild it. This was all at the builders cost but we still had the delay to the build.

The spatial redesigning required a total of 26 new steel beams to allow for the adjustment of the levels of the ground and first floors while lifting the roof to add an extra floor. To compensate for the absence of initial outdoor space, we carved out amenity areas at the rear by cutting back into the building. Design elements like industrial-style aluminium windows were carefully chosen to restore the building's industrial character, creating a look that was both unique and sensitive to the property's heritage. We also prioritised the restoration of original features like the flint wall and chimney to not only preserve, but enhance elements of heritage value. This was key as the site is located within a conservation area, but these elements are often not straightforward and needed a well skilled team to deliver them correctly.

Undoubtedly, one of the reasons we were successful in delivering this project was via continual professional monitoring of the site, and by maintaining good and open communication with all parties at all times. There was plenty of effort and time spent through the process to ensure that the build progressed according to the timeline, and to the design and spec we had set out.

www.sustainomics.co.uk

My favourite part of the build was when we had removed the roof and were up on the scaffolding at the new top floor roof height and realised that we could see the sea! We hadn't expected this as we were surrounded by buildings and it prompted an excited review of the plans with the builder. We

ended up changing the layout of the top two flats so that each lounge could take advantage of the sea views!

We finished all the flats to a very high spec, definitely the nicest in the area. We aimed for the top 5 % of the market. It was fantastic to walk around the finished flats, seeing the vision brought to life.

Our strategy is to convert commercial buildings, and keep for the long-term, so all of our deals are built with an intent to remortgage as an exit and hold to rent out.

Financials

Purchase price - £405k

Refurb costs - £591k

End Valuation - £1.9m

We funded the deal completely through private investors, and after acquiring the term finance upon completion of the flats, we were able to repay our investors plus their interest, and create a nice profit margin for ourselves to withdraw from the deal.

The Rock Factory was the first commercial conversion we had done together as a company and really proved the model for us; it gave us confidence to continue to build out other schemes. It also gave our investors confidence that we could, and would, do as we had promised. All of our initial investors have reinvested in us for another year.

Key lessons

- Work with great people who have complimentary, but different, skills to your own

- Have multiple fallback positions - aim for the best case in deal analysis but always understand and plan for what would happen in the worst case scenario

- Spend time and energy on planning applications and planning committees

- Ensure that the builder specs are high quality, comprehensive and detailed. We spent a lot of time through the build where the builder would claim a variation but we were able to go back to the drawings and original spec and prove that it was always in the original spec

- Design a high-quality product that you are proud of - it feels fantastic once it is finished and the valuer will love it too!

At Arcvelop, we strive for excellence in every facet of our work, always seeking to elevate our developments beyond expectations. Our core principles are: exceptional design, intelligent use of materials, restoration of traditional features, and meticulous craftsmanship. These principles guide us in creating developments that fuse heritage and innovation, resulting in an aesthetic appeal that is both unique and fitting to its surroundings.

Our strategy is to focus on repurposing underutilised or dilapidated commercial/mixed use buildings and converting them to high quality residential apartment blocks to hold for the long-term.

We typically target properties we can develop into less than ten units. By staying beneath this threshold, we avoid affordable homes contributions, which can slow down the planning process. This strategy streamlines our operations, leading to quicker turnovers and more efficient project completion, and we feel this suits our risk appetite better than larger schemes.

Where possible we also look to capitalise on the Permitted Development Rights that commercial buildings often hold. This reduces the planning risk and accelerates timelines, facilitates a smoother transition from commercial to residential use and accelerating our project turnover.

Our approach to these types of projects allows us to blend aesthetic, financial, environmental and societal benefits, whilst at the same time creating good investment opportunities. These revitalised buildings then benefit local communities by adding to vitality, and we have found if done right, this can be a very rewarding feeling on a local level.

We currently have a conversion of an old Motor cycle shop to 10 Flats in Norwich underway, an office to residential conversion in Kent that will convert a 30,000sqft office to 40 flats and have just completed on a 20 unit scheme in Sheffield. We are excited to continue to provide great quality accommodation to tenants for years to come.

FROM STRENGTH TO STRENGTH – KEVIN EDGE

"Our built environment is the physical reflection of our collective dreams, aspirations, and achievements" – Lucas Donovan

Introduction

I started my working life as a Bricklayer, but I was ambitious and quite quickly elevated to managing extensions and smaller builds. My entrepreneurial spirit soon had me wanting to be more involved in the business side of the industry and a step up to property development was a natural progression for me. Utilising my skills and knowledge gave me the confidence and experience to pursue and complete large developments of currently up to £10m GDV.

In the competitive landscape of property development, the transformation of a simple structure into a profitable HMO in St. Albans is a clear-cut case of identifying and capitalizing on a market need. This project was driven by a straightforward objective - to develop a property that meets the high demand for quality accommodation in prime commuter belt.

My background in construction and property development has always been geared towards pragmatic and strategic project selection. This development in St. Albans was a calculated decision, informed by experience and an understanding of the local property market potential. It was a move to tap into the underserved sector of the housing market, with a focus on creating value and return on investment. It also allowed me an income that relieved the pressure of day-to-day business within the build side of my Company.

The concept for this development was rooted in practicality and the recognition of St. Albans as an area ripe for high-yield property ventures. The city's proximity to London and its own local amenities made it an ideal location for developing an HMO that would appeal to professionals commuting to the capital and those looking for quality local living options.

This project was not about grand visions or personal missions; it was business, pure and simple. It was about taking a well-located, but underperforming property, and turning it into a highly desirable living space. The process was as much about construction and design as it was about understanding and meeting the needs of the target market.

As a result, this project stands as a successful chapter in my career as a developer and as a model for efficient and profitable property development. It is a testament to the power of market research, financial acumen, and solid execution in the field of property development.

Where did it all begin?

The project began with a tip from a trusted local agent, a relationship cultivated over years of honest feedback and reliable dealings. This connection proved invaluable, leading to the acquisition of a site with untapped potential in a prime commuter location.

Market Research and Financial Analysis

In-depth market research revealed a gap in the local market for quality HMOs within proximity to St. Albans mainline railway station. Financial projections favoured the conversion of existing flats into mini-HMOs, promising a higher return on investment. The financial breakdown is as follows:

Financial Metric	Amount (£)
Purchase Price	£525,000
Conversion Costs	£265,000
Legals and SDLT	£20,000
Finance Costs	£55,000
Total Cost	**£865,000**
Valuation at Aug 16	£1,720,000
Profit	£855,000
Cashflow (After Refinance)	
Projected Income per Month	£9,000
Expenses	£4,200
Profit	£4,800
ROCE %	Infinite

Financing the Project

The project was financed through private investor funds which enabled us to purchase the property outright. This approach was instrumental in the project's inception, as it allowed for a 'no-money-down' acquisition, enhancing the financial leverage and potential returns.

Strategy and Execution

We collaborated with a trusted investor, with whom we had a history of successful projects, and were introduced to a new investor through a reliable contact. This network of investors believed in the potential of the project and provided the necessary funds to purchase the building in cash.

Outcome

Upon completion of the development, we executed a refinancing strategy that not only facilitated the full repayment to our investors but also secured a substantial profit for the company. This financial model proved to be highly effective, making the project exceptionally profitable and reinforcing the company's reputation for delivering lucrative investment opportunities.

Project Challenges

Challenge 1: Working adjacent to an occupied block and near a train line

One of the primary challenges was conducting the development work adjacent to a fully occupied block of flats. This proximity meant that any external work had to be executed with minimal disruption to the residents. We also had to be considerate of the neighbourhood's infrastructure, which included negotiating the temporary use of parking spaces to create a small compound for our operations.

Moreover, the close vicinity to the train line added a layer of complexity to the project. It was imperative to always maintain a clean and orderly site. A stray piece of debris on the tracks could lead to significant delays and financial penalties. The safety protocols mandate stopping trains at the slightest hint of potential danger could result in very big fines!

Solution

To address these challenges, we implemented stringent site management protocols. A clear communication plan was established with the residents of the adjacent flats to inform them of our work schedule and any potential inconveniences. We took extra measures to secure the site, ensuring that all materials and waste were managed effectively to prevent any from reaching the railway lines.

Our team were briefed on the importance of maintaining a tidy environment, and regular checks were conducted to uphold these standards. By fostering a culture of vigilance and respect for our surroundings, we managed to keep the project on track, without incident, and maintained a good relationship with our neighbours, which was as crucial to our success as the development work itself.

www.sustainomics.co.uk

Challenge 2: Navigating Planning and Regulatory Hurdles for Unlicensed HMOs

A significant challenge in property development is ensuring regulatory compliance, especially when innovating with property use. For this project, we identified an opportunity to develop mini-HMOs within the existing flats, which fell under the category of unlicensed HMOs. This meant that while we were exempt from the need for a formal HMO license, we still had to adhere to stringent fire, welfare, and safety standards.

Solution

Leveraging our property education and understanding of local regulations, we capitalized on the unlicensed HMO opportunity to maximize the project's value. Our approach involved a thorough analysis of the regulatory framework to ensure full compliance with all necessary standards, without the need for a license.

We maintained open communication with the local authorities, presenting our innovative use of space and demonstrating how it aligned with safety and welfare requirements. This strategy not only facilitated a smoother planning process but also allowed us to enhance the project's profitability and viability.

By staying informed and prepared, we turned what could have been a complex regulatory navigation into a value-creation strategy, showcasing our ability to adapt and innovate within the development sector.

Challenge 3: High Standards within Budget Constraints

Achieving high standards within budget constraints was a critical challenge. Our objective was to offer a premium living experience that didn't come with an exorbitant price tag, ensuring the project remained financially viable.

Solution

Our approach to maintaining cost-effectiveness, without sacrificing quality, involved meticulous financial planning and management. We adopted a rigorous cost-control regime, carefully evaluating every quote and opting to purchase materials in bulk, where feasible. Innovative construction techniques were also employed to minimise labour costs while ensuring quality remained uncompromised.

One key observation that gave us a competitive edge was the property's robust construction quality - the building being a modern structure with high quality standards of build and detailing. The generous floor-to-ceiling heights provided us with the flexibility needed for efficient planning of drainage and services. The presence of concrete floors, especially on the first floor, offered a solid and durable foundation for our development work.

The contemporary build quality meant the construction process was not only straightforward but also predictable. The modern compliance with building regulations ensured that there were fewer hidden surprises, which is a common issue with older properties. This predictability in the building's condition allowed us to plan with greater accuracy and reduced the risk of unforeseen expenses, ensuring the project's smooth execution within the set budget.

Challenge 4: Ensuring Tenant Satisfaction and Retention

In the competitive HMO market, achieving tenant satisfaction is crucial for long-term success. It was essential for us to create a property that not only attracted residents but also inspired them to make it their long-term home.

Solution

Our strategy for fostering tenant satisfaction involved more than just the physical design of the property; it was about cultivating a sense of community and belonging. We designed the spaces with an emphasis on creating 'homes' rather than 'units', integrating communal areas and private sanctuaries within each apartment. We also established a proactive communication system to address tenant concerns swiftly, ensuring their comfort and well-being were always at the forefront.

The property's prime location, in close proximity to the town centre and train station, significantly contributed to tenant retention. This convenience, coupled with our commitment to maintaining high-quality living spaces, has been instrumental in our success. We took pride in the size and quality of the rooms we offered, which have consistently met the needs of our tenants, providing them with spacious and comfortable living conditions. As a result, we have been fortunate to have tenants choose to stay with us for extended periods, affirming the value and appeal of our properties.

Key Learnings

1. The Importance of Strategic Relationships

Building and maintaining strong relationships with investors, local authorities, and contractors is crucial. These relationships can lead to new opportunities, smoother project execution, and potential for future collaboration.

2. Effective Communication is Key

Keeping open lines of communication with all stakeholders, including neighbours, tenants, and team members, is essential. It ensures that everyone is informed, reduces conflicts, and fosters a collaborative environment.

3. Adaptability in Project Management

Being able to adapt to unforeseen challenges, such as working next to a train line or within a busy residential area, is vital.

Clear project management and contingency planning can mitigate risks and prevent costly delays.

4. Financial Foresight and Planning

Understanding the financial landscape and planning accordingly, from sourcing funds to managing costs and executing a refinancing strategy, is a cornerstone of successful property development.

5. Quality and Detailing in Construction

Recognising the potential in properties with high-quality construction and detailing can lead to more predictable and straightforward development processes. This foresight can result in fewer surprises and a smoother project timeline.

Conclusion

This project in St. Albans stands as a testament to strategic market analysis, astute financial planning, and the execution of high-quality development projects. It shows how a clear vision, coupled with rigorous project management and a keen understanding of investor relations, can result in a successful commercial venture that meets the growing demand for quality housing needs.

The completion of this development not only solidified our position in the market but also highlighted our ability to navigate complex regulatory environments and logistical challenges. By converting a conventional building into a series of

mini-HMOs, we have maximized the property's value and utility, reflecting our commitment to innovation and strong financial controls.

As we move forward, the knowledge and experience gained from this project will inform our approach to future developments. We remain focused on identifying lucrative opportunities that promise substantial returns for our investors and our company. The success of this project reinforces our confidence in our business model and in our ability to deliver exceptional results within the competitive landscape of property development.

With each project, we refine our methods and sharpen our competitive edge, ensuring that we continue to identify and develop properties that not only promise, but deliver significant investment rewards. As we conclude this chapter, we look to the future with anticipation for the next venture, ready

to take on new opportunities and achieve further successes in property development.

We have moved into housebuilding as well now, taking our learnings to the next level. What we love about working in property is the opportunity for constant growth as a business, while serving the needs of the housing market and offering real value to people's lives!

UNLOCKING POTENTIAL: A JOURNEY TO COMMERCIAL CONVERSIONS, INSPIRED BY PERSONAL CHALLENGES – BJORN HARRIS

"If you can't always change the cards you are dealt, change how you play your hand" - Randy Pausch

My story starts years before our first commercial conversion and without these chain of events, I wouldn't be here contributing to this book and sharing my experiences.

So many times the hardest step starting something new is having the confidence and a drive that prioritises your focus. For me, this came from a clear "Why".

For 15 years, I was so fortunate to be part of a leading global electronics Japanese Organisation. Working at the European Headquarters, I spent years embedded in large-scale transformation projects, defining and delivering strategy and driving change. Initially starting out managing small teams to finally leading European Business Units, the skill sets that came with the career journey were invaluable. I was fortunate to be dealt such a hand. However, my biggest challenge came in my personal life when our eldest son was born and shortly after his birth, we started our new journey. Ben was born with an acute syndrome with life-long cognitive and physical challenges.

As a family, we had to adapt quickly and learn to manage our new norm. Balancing work, career and Ben's care and support was a challenge and it became clear that this wasn't sustainable for the long-term. The stresses that came with the work and the long hours didn't align with the needs of family life.

We knew we couldn't change the cards we were dealt, but it was time to change how we would play them.

In 2019, my wife and I sat down to develop a Family Vision and Strategy. We knew we needed to make some big changes to ensure Ben's well-being, achieve work-life balance, structure our finances, and also to support causes that had helped us with Ben over the years. So, using the strategies and experience from corporate life, we set out our next three-five year plan.

The First Card is played

"If you can't see yourself working with someone for life, don't work with them for a day." Naval Ravikant

We explored different avenues for securing financial security, identifying areas where our acquired skills would be transferable. We landed on property as being a significant part of our future wealth management strategy and over the course of two years, we purchased and developed several residential to HMO conversions, which allowed freedom to transition from corporate into property full time. But it was the chance dinner conversation I had with an old friend which opened up the next stage in property; realising our investment strategies and investment locations were similar, we begun to foster a great trust-based relationship utilising the same network of partners.

An Ace up our sleeve

It was this close collaboration between us, and also with our partners, that brought about the first commercial to residential opportunity. We recognised that our chosen town on the south coast of England provided a great opportunity for enhancing and converting existing developments. The town is surrounded by the protected downland of a National Park - the sea to the south, and the boundary, with a neighbouring District to the north and east and much of the land through the central area is functional floodplain. These physical and environmental constraints limit the amount of land that is available to develop. As such, the town does not have sufficient land to meet development needs in full, even at significantly increased densities, and this was a perfect backdrop for our strategy and working with the local council in supporting their future planning strategy.

Seizing the Hand - Opportunity knocks

Through our network of contacts, we were alerted to a distressed commercial conversion opportunity. A joint venture had gone sour, and the partners were eager to sell the property quickly.

The property was an old Guest House by the coast with planning permission for conversion to residential. We saw the potential to add significant value to the end product, and we were keen to act fast.

With secured funds using a blend of our own money and private loans, a cash purchase offer, a four-week exchange, and a team of experienced professionals who would take over the refurbishment, we were able to demonstrate credibility and commitment to delivering on our promises.

Our offer was accepted, and we completed on the property within six weeks of the offer.

The Development – how it played out

The development conversion went smoothly, with the plans largely following the original approved plans from the previous owners, transforming it from its current C1 class to C3. This allowed us to keep the project fairly simple and get straight to work on converting the property into one three-bed terraced property dwelling, two sizeable three-bed apartments, and one standalone cottage.

The timeline from purchase to completion was just under 11 months. Although we experienced some cost creep from the work required for upgrading electricity and gas supplies into

the properties, and some cost increase due to upgrading the rooms for the apartments, we were able to absorb these costs from our contingency fund and from the increased rental income as a result of the upgraded rooms.

One of the aspects that made this project such a useful step-ping stone into commercial conversions was having planning permission in place as part of the sale. This significantly reduced our risk and allowed us to visualise additional oppor-tunities and value add to the scheme, without delaying the overall project.

High Stakes - Adding Value Through Strategic Thinking

In addition to the value of converting the property from commercial to residential use, we also implemented a number of strategic initiatives to further increase the value of our investment.

Title splitting: This gave greater flexibility in terms of our exit strategy and increased the overall valuation of the property.

Phased delivery: By structuring the build work more effectively, we were able to deliver the project in phases, which kick-started rental income generation early, improving cash flow. This reduced the risk that many commercial developments have of seeing profit being generated only at the very end.

Tax efficiency: We negotiated the terms of the sale based on a residential sale Stamp Duty Land Tax (SDLT) calculation. This was a cashflow advantage as we made savings by reclaiming some of the SDLT after the sale.

Layout optimisation: By changing our end strategy of renting as residential Buy To Let apartments, we added a stage to the process with permitted development to HMOs, thus maximizing rental income significantly. Our scope change came in the form of also changing some of the rooms to studios, providing better living spaces for tenants who desire shared living whilst enjoying sufficient privacy.

Early marketing: We marketed the last and biggest phase of the development early on, working closely with our management agent to generate interest through an open day and social media. Implementing early-stage property marketing proved instrumental, translating to rapid tenant occupation.

Hitting the Jackpot - Financial Rewards and Long-Term Impact

In navigating the financial landscape of our project, a measured approach has always been our guiding principle.

The conversion of this property into four high-quality residential units yielded a Gross Development Value (GDV) of £1.3 million, which generated a 21% profit margin. However, our strategy, anchored in the pursuit of long-term intergenerational wealth, steered us towards a more conservative path and opting for a long-term hold.

This deliberate choice offers a recurring net rental income of £82,000 per year after factoring all costs.

Dealing the Building Blocks for Success

"Be Smart. No one cares about your efforts. Only your results."
Naval Ravikant

So, what would be the key advances that this one project has added to my personal and professional growth?

This will be a modest sized commercial development project in comparison to the other authors of this book, but I firmly believe making your goals and targets accessible and focussing on working smart for your first project – or in any new realm - helps to add to your confidence for future success. If I go back through my past, it certainly holds true. In earlier Corporate life, when I couldn't see a good career path after being in the same management position for five years, it took time to build confidence to switch to another part of the organisation but this opened up so many new avenues. Or where you open yourself up to potential scrutiny and failure when implementing organisational changes that are deeply opposed by individuals – it feels daunting at first but breaking it down into smaller wins helps it succeed. In property, it was our first HMO conversion that felt like such a hurdle to overcome but once we got the results, it developed the confidence to continue the property journey. The repeated theme here is our first building block to success:

1) **Self-belief, Work smart and Build confidence**

2) **Connections, Partnerships, People**

In Corporate, you define roles and responsibilities for every employee but in a small business you simply cannot deliver everything on your own. Alongside the impracticalities of not having the qualifications or experience, it would be ineffective. Our strategy has been to outsource key parts of the process to professionals. This means that our Joint Venture can dedicate time on the core of the business – including Strategy, Future Business Development, Operational Efficiency and Business Control.

Relying on great partnerships and others experience is absolutely crucial in defining your own business success and results. These took time to nurture and we set a foundation in place through the earlier projects, gaining mutual trust and by aligning our key values with those we work with:

Integrity | Partnership | Excellence

Further, I would extend this to non-direct partnerships – those not working directly on the project but have an influence on your success. These include mentors, mastermind groups and relationships with other successful developers.

3) **Brand, Strategy and Direction.** This project helped to outline our business and company structure, and assisted us to define our Brand, Strategy and Direction.

Our company name originated from this first project, as the Guest House was called Bella Vista. Meaning 'beautiful view' in Italian, it is a reflection of our vision to create beautiful views for every finished product.

4) **Adding Value.** Again, a parallel to Corporate life was to always instil value-add in any delivery coming from the team and demonstrating a team's value and purpose to stay relevant within the organisation's strategy. I can see the importance now as well within property development. Firstly, to ensure that you are competitive, stand out and 'win' future potential development opportunities – which can come from the value you can add to a development - but also to deliver additional value to your project financials, to the tenants, and

having a shared value approach with the team you work with. This creates such a great win-win culture.

And lastly, invest in great photography and/or CGI photos throughout the property development. Investing in them once means you have them forever - to use for so many beneficial purposes - including in this book. We did not and it is one addition we will now invest in for all future projects!

The Next Move

As we plan our path forward, the essence of our family goals remain rooted with time being our greatest measure of wealth. Our professional ambitions continue to focus on future commercial developments. We are currently converting an old care home into nine apartments, picking up new learnings and facing new challenges and will continue to find new projects that align with our company vision, whilst embracing the philosophy that 'small is beautiful' and not racing for larger developments. This will allow us to navigate the intricate landscape of opportunities with agility and focused growth.

TRANSFORMING BUILDINGS, ENHANCING LIVES – GILES HARRISON AND NANA BANTON

"It is the most simple of gestures that make the most significant differences" - Maya Yamanouchi

A good developer breathes new life into the property they've acquired, curating its 'reincarnation'.

A *great* property developer looks beyond the bricks and mortar and prepares to inspire fresh life in the *people* who will inhabit their building.

To be clear, we don't think property developers are life-giving Gods. We do believe, however, that property developers have the great privilege and responsibility to powerfully impact people's lives. Well-developed properties are places to call home, to meet, to debate, rest, work and play. They can become places of protection, provision and empowerment. With such responsibility comes the question - *what could property development achieve if at the heart of the strategy was the aim to support individuals (who often cannot easily find properties that meet their needs), to create a home where they can thrive?* That's what we, Nana and Giles, the co-directors of Abacus Fairhomes, are finding out. Together, we're not just transforming buildings; we're on a mission to enhance lives too.

We met at a Commercial Conversion seminar in 2019 and discovered that we had similar values and attitude to property. Neither of us felt property investment was just about striving for maximum profit. We both wanted to invest in a legacy which also benefits others.

At that time, I (Giles) had recently left my job, after 16 years at the BBC. I was working as a freelance TV producer and director and wanted to step into a new chapter of my career.

Nana – whose professional background is in consultancy, leadership and change management – had recently set up a care company and was looking for ways to create homes for Supported Living. *(Supported Living is a service which supports someone with additional care needs. For example, a Supported Living placement might enable an autistic adult to live in a self-contained flat and receive support from professionals to live with greater independence.)* Nana had a captivating vision for change. Life and work had exposed her to the difficulties vulnerable people face in being supported in (and by) their own community. She wanted to be part of an integrated solution, where people not only receive a suitable package of care, but do so from a home which truly supports their needs *and* grants accessibility to the community in which they belong.

It was clear we each felt that property offered a great opportunity for solid business *and* the potential for positive social impact.

After several months of keeping in touch, we bumped into each other at an auction viewing for a shop and uppers. At this stage we each had small property portfolios comprising mainly of BTL/HMOs, but both attended the auction with a view to convert the uppers for some form of care/Supported Living. Now knowing each other's motivation for developing, we said, "Why don't we buy it together?" - and just like that, the business was born. Well, perhaps not *just* like that! Although we didn't know it at the time, it was a good job we did *not* in fact buy our first joint property at that March 2020 auction. The Covid lockdowns were spent devising and refining our business plan, getting to grips with what we wanted to do - how, where and *why*.

The Current Project

In July 2020, we bought our first property - a vacant former workshop/store in Twickenham, South West London. At 215sqm (2,300 sq ft) over two floors, we felt it wasn't too large for a first project. The building would become a block of flats for vulnerable adults – each living in their own, custom-designed home – supported to grow in independence, and empowered to flourish in the community. We worked out a GDV based on residential sales values and estimated the cost of conversion to give us a maximum bid price, which we would fund with a mixture of our own cash and a bridge loan. When the time came, we secured the property – via online auction, due to the pandemic – well below our ceiling price.

Stage 1 – Planning

No matter how aspirational or compassionate the motivation for our work, we were always going to face challenges.

Our first attempt at securing Permitted Development (PD) was rejected by the council, in part because we hadn't given enough evidence of the property's existing use. With this in mind we went back to the drawing board and, with the help of our new planning consultant, submitted a pre-app. We had always *intended* to apply for full planning; extending into the roof would enable us to create an extra flat and a nice communal area (with roof terrace) for the residents. But our pre-app submission brought to the fore two significant challenges. Firstly, the officer implied that extending into the roof would only happen over his dead body - not a good look for a company striving for a life-enhancing legacy! Secondly, it was made clear that he considered this building valuable employment space, and that the council would strongly resist losing it.

Abandoning our dream of an extra flat and beautiful rooftop was one of those sacrifices we'd learnt to become familiar with (as all developers do). Now, we would just convert the existing building and instead focus on convincing the officer that this uninsulated and abandoned building was not, in fact, valuable employment space.

Our research led to some strong arguments:

- The property had generated zero jobs during the past ten years, whereas our residential use would generate 8-12 local, full-time equivalent jobs.

- In the last 50 years, no commercial tenant had remained at the property for longer than ten years (and most a lot less) and we had established with the Local Authority's Social Care Team that there was strong demand for Supported Living in the borough.

- Importantly, we also proved that the property's use class was not protected under the Local Plan & Article 4 (because it had never been used as an office).

Nevertheless, there was still strong resistance from the planners. It was only when we suggested a planning condition that the permission was unlocked; the property's use would be restricted to Supported Living. It was refreshing to find that the exit that we *actually wanted* was the key to permission being granted!

It took 11 months to secure the permission, and a further five months to agree the associated s106 legal agreement. The permission was formally granted in April 2022.

Stage 2 – Funding the Build

Nana and I used the time, while negotiating the s106, to also proceed with a detailed design. At this stage, the unique challenges of the building became apparent. Every single surface needed insulating (thanks to the property's solid brick, single-pane windows and asbestos-ridden roof). Consequently, a large part of the fabric of the building needed to be replaced. Our envisaged budget of £350k started looking more like £500k.

From the start, the residents that would occupy the space (theoretical, at this stage) were at the forefront of our thinking, but the truth is the obstacles were increasing – and it was tricky. Our first Quantity Surveyor retired, so a new one took over the tender process. Suitable contractors were shortlisted and invited to tender; to our shock, the returned tendered prices ranged from £640,000 - £1.4m! We set about re-designing the scheme (removing a small-cantilevered extension at first floor) in an attempt to reduce costs by about £100k.

The re-design cost us time and money and required another planning submission (smoother sailing this time). Painfully, the new tender bids were not so different to those which had previously shocked us. This was, after all, a time of skyrocketing material costs, labour shortages and economic uncertainty. We decided to look beyond the tender process and we were very grateful to secure a decent-sized contractor, whose scale and great track record gave us confidence they would see their way through the turmoil. What's more, they proposed doing the project on a procurement management basis with a Guaranteed Maximum Price (GMP). This means that rather than being a fixed-price main contractor (where their profit – and risk – is built into the price) they would sit 'on our side' as consultants and manage all the subcontractors, with an open book policy. We agreed a target price up front and any saving below that, we'd share. It was ideal - experience, quality, cost-savings and reduced risk.

Then the funding went awry. Although they had been comfortable with the GMP, the bank's Monitoring Surveyor incorporated excessively high contingency into the budget, which took the project over the bank's lending criteria. The lender pulled out just before Christmas 2022, but thankfully our resilient finance broker secured another source of development finance. That came with various strings attached – which ultimately led us to engage a new contractor. At last, we were set to go!

Now, knee-deep in the build phase, we are being expertly guided by our wonderful architect who is also acting as contract administrator. There will no doubt be other problems along the way or as we like to put it 'opportunities for finding solutions!' - no-one ever said development was easy (and if they did, they're lying!), but we still believe in our purpose, and once we deliver these homes, it will all be worth it.

Reflections

At several points throughout the journey the obstacles have seemed insurmountable. More than once we've asked ourselves, "should we just sell up?". But each time, we've decided that seeing the project through would enable us to continue learning, and that is exactly what has happened. As we look to the future and plan for a much bigger project (perhaps ten to fifteen flats), we can reflect on the challenges faced in our first project and recognise the value of our newly found problem-solving solutions.

Above all, we've not given up because of the shared vision which first brought Nana and I together. We're not in it simply to transform buildings, or purely to bolster our bank balances. We are driven by the positive social impact of what we do. Our commitment to developing this property to the best of its (and our) capability can, and will, literally transform the lives of vulnerable individuals. We can, and will, continue to work with local authorities, landlords and other developers (for whom – by the way – we offer an excellent exit opportunity) to re-purpose buildings that will enhance community access, support unique physical and emotional needs, create an environment for meaningful connection, provide safety and comfort, and accelerate the quest for independence to often denied vulnerable adults.

Very soon, our vision for this once-neglected Twickenham warehouse is set to become a reality. Practical completion is due in early 2024 and the care provider (Nana's company, Abacus Care & Support) is already in conversation with Local

Authorities about possible tenants. The property we have developed into Supported Living accommodation – through labour and love – will soon be home to vulnerable adults receiving the support they truly need and deserve.

A few bumps in the road here and there - 100% worth it.

Lessons Learned

Our five top tips sum up our lessons learned:

1. Learn from others. Talk, listen and read in order to learn from others. There is almost certainly someone who has worked through the obstacle you're facing before. Learn from their successes *and* mistakes.

2. Take action. There's only so much you can learn in theory, you've got to get stuck in. Immersing yourself in the process is the only way your experience will grow.

3. Be prepared for challenges. Accepting that challenges will arise can help you not to become overwhelmed. Remember, each challenge is an opportunity for successful problem solving. Having a great professional team will help you to navigate and weather the challenges.

4. Persevere. It may not be quite how you imagined, but more times than not, there is a solution to the problem you're facing. *Expect* to overcome and keep on keeping on.

5. Believe in yourself! It sounds clichéd but if you believe, you really can achieve. We're not dismissing the fact that skill, research, collaboration and – let's face it – luck, have an awfully big part to play. But trusting that you *can* get to the finishing line goes a long way to preparing yourself for the journey - if your belief wavers (as it does for all of us at some time or

another), seek out trusted sources who believe in you. They can help guide you back to the path of believing in yourself.

ENJOYING
THE DEVELOPMENT RIDE
– LUCY AND STEPHANIE INGRAM

'Whether you think you can, or you think you can't -
you're right' – Henry Ford

Life before property

Before we became property investors our life was simple. It was about finding the next adventure, whether that be travelling to the mountains or the sea in our van, and riding sideways in the pow or on a wave. We had a blast!

But between each adventure we both had full-time jobs in the Royal Navy - not just your average 9-5. This was also a job that brought us adventure - being whisked away to far strung places around the globe, at the drop of a hat, can be a lot of fun in early adulthood. But as you get more, let's say, mature, you start to covet stability and certainty - two things the military is not.

So as time went on and our military careers progressed we started to acknowledge that our time together was just way too brief - we were the typical military 'weekend warriors', always rushing 'up the line' (home) for a mere 36 hours that seemed to fly past in the blink of an eye and, before we knew it, it was Sunday and we were packing bags, ready to do it all again.

The discontent really began in 2018 when Steph was deployed to the Far East for a whole year, and I had suffered a significant shoulder injury while competing at the British Snowboard champs. We started to think that something had to give. I was facing what seemed like an endless pathway to recovery and Steph was halfway across the world - this wasn't how we wanted to live. We had great, secure jobs, a healthy six figure income and loads of benefits, but what good was this without each other? We had spent the majority of our relationship, and now marriage, separated in space (and often time!). We wanted more from our combined existence and so we began exploring alternative wealth building strategies in an attempt to unlock a future together that gave us our time back.

In our goal of replacing my military income, we started out in buy-to-lets before exploring more creative strategies and moving into Rent-2-Rent. We immediately identified with this strategy, in particular how there was a well-trodden path to getting out of the start gate and, with little capital required upfront, your only barrier to success is the effort you are willing to put in. So, we put our heads down and took positive action, every day, until we had built up nearly 50 'professional' HMO and Serviced Accommodation (SA) units within six months.

The project

We secured our first major 'commercial to resi' development project through Rightmove in spring 2021. 'Townsend House', a vast period property in Plymouth, was our real property awakening. It was a care home dating back to 1832 and, at nearly 500 sqm and set in a third of an acre of beautiful grounds, it had planning permission to convert into six apartments and a separate coach house dwelling. This was exactly what we had been looking for!

Nevertheless, our development experience to date consisted of '2up-2down' refurbs - we had no construction knowledge, no build team and knew nothing of commercial finance, VAT, and the rest. The fear was real, but we felt it and did it anyway.

So how did we get the offer accepted? It wasn't rocket science! We were open and honest with the agent from the beginning, being fully transparent about our (lack of) experience in commercial conversions and focused on demonstrating our strengths - motivation, work ethic, integrity, courage - what we would call our 'military mindset'! Over a number of visits we built a solid rapport with the agent and, after we finally had our offer accepted he informed us it was because of our 'likeability' and 'trust' that he put us forward as the preferred buyer, despite many other more experienced developers being in the mix. It's the age-old adage that people won't remember what you said, but they will remember how you made them feel.

We used a mixture of development finance and private investment to fund the scheme, which took 12 months to complete. With Steph still full-time military at this point, I can only say I was in my element every day - creating new business relationships, attracting investors, building the power team, engaging with stakeholders and managing the project.

Don't get me wrong - it isn't all rosy in developments! There were highs and lows a plenty, and with only two months to go we found ourselves in a place no developer wants to find themselves - we had no choice but to let our builders go. This left us with only two options - give up, or make it work and finish the commercial conversion project ourselves. And if my time in the services had taught me anything, it was how routine, consistency, teamwork and embracing challenges are

key attributes to achieving success. So, I gathered together a new team in a matter of days and rolled my sleeves up (literally), taking on the role of principal contractor, project manager AND pretty much full-time labourer, painter, chippie, cleaner and the rest to get the project over the line. All this at the most challenging phase of the project, oh and of course with Steph informing me she was deploying to the Baltics for the final five weeks!

That whole final chapter was all a bit of a blur. In hindsight it was probably the most physically and mentally demanding period I've ever been through. BUT it is times like this when you have a decision to make - do I give up, or do I keep going? I chose the latter, ensuring I mustered the right people around me to share the love (and pain), and persevered every day until completion. Ultimately we managed to deliver a scheme which exceeded the original GDV by 15%. There is no better feeling than moving in excited new homeowners, espe-

cially after such challenges had been faced and overcome. One sale did later fall through due to a change in circumstances by the buyer, and so we made the decision to keep it ourselves (which happened to be the penthouse with sea-

views!) for our own portfolio, which is now run as a very successful serviced accommodation apartment.

Even when things were particularly challenging, I still knew I was exactly where I wanted to be in life and that made it 'easier' to get up each day and keep doing it. Property development is my 'ikigai' down to a tea - that intersection of what you love, what you are good at, what the world needs and what you can be paid for. These overlapping circles create your passion, profession, mission and vocation. If you can find something that sits in the centre of the Venn diagram, you are winning in life - and I had found it!

Throughout the project, I tried my best to consistently document the journey in a very transparent, honest and relatable way. Social media has kept me accountable and gave me a platform to demonstrate the realities and associated risks of leading a construction project.

One thing that has been frequently pointed out to me is how I manage as a gender minority in a very male-dominated industry. In my many years in the military, as a minority, I would say the main thing I've identified is that generally women lack the self-belief against their male-counterparts of the same skill level. On that, we have two quotes on our living room wall at home - the first is Henry Ford's 'whether you think you can or you can't, you are right' and the second is simply 'You got this!' And I can say that both of these were referred to on numerous occasions during the project! I have certainly found that by applying a confident, forward-thinking, and open-minded approach, it has allowed me to forge some incredible working relationships which have enabled me to extract the very best of my team and deliver the project.

Noting my limited experience in the construction industry, my advice to other female developers or would-be developers is "Be confident, have courage, don't take any BS and, most importantly, be yourself."- I've found authenticity is what people respect. I hope through documenting my journey that I have encouraged aspiring female property developers to take the leap of faith and become ambitious action takers. I invest a lot of time engaging with women who have reached out and are eager to learn about what it takes to make the transition into Property Development; going forward I am passionate about continuing to network and collaborate with other driven female and male entrepreneurs. I believe there is huge potential for women to add real value in the construction sector – all that is required is the right mindset, putting one foot in front of the other and taking consistent action daily!

Our top three

If we had to draw out the three biggest lessons from our first meander into commercial conversions, they would be: invest in your marketing, get the right people around you, and dare I say it, trust no one! Below we have tried to capture the reasons why these are lessons that are super important for developers to take onboard:

1. Invest in your marketing - early!

The power and importance of investing in high quality professional marketing cannot be underestimated. As well as having professional marketing videos, glossy brochures and dazzling CGIs created, we also took the decision to create a show flat and run a 'muddy boots' open day fairly early on. This was a great success, leading to six out of the seven sales secured.

The marketing strategies all proved instrumental in creating a buzz and achieving sales at the recommended prices and above. It is also important to note that great marketing products become company assets - we have used the CGIs, photography and videos created on multiple occasions for further marketing purposes, to demonstrate credibility in the industry and to attract further company investment.

2. The right professional team is priceless

Having a solid power team around you is fundamental to any development project. When we look back at our initial venture, into the world of property development, we shudder at the thought of what we didn't know or fully appreciate. If we'd been a bit more aware of some of the aspects of compliance beforehand, this could have saved important mind space for all the other complexities that running a development project ultimately brings! Thankfully, through ensuring we had incredible professionals in our wider team to guide and assist us (and constantly asking the dumb questions), this helped enormously in keeping us on the right side of development compliance.

When purchasing a site, you need to ensure you are structured in the right way to enable your chosen exit. For us, we initially went in with the goal of holding the apartments, but quickly changed our mind based on market conditions and our specific goals at that time. The buying entity needs to align with the exit strategy, but all possible scenarios must be thoroughly thought through with a Plan B (and even a Plan C) in the back pocket. Changing strategies halfway through could have significant tax implications when it comes to your exit in areas such as VAT. All this must be planned and coordinated appropriately with professional advice from the right accountant and tax advisor, so ensure you have professionals around you that specialise in developments from the outset. This way, you avoid the nasty surprise of huge tax bills at the end of your project which can easily eat into your well-earned profit!

3. Trust no one?

Unfortunately, there is no one single aspect of due diligence that will provide a panacea of protection during a development - instead we recommend pursuing a vigilant approach that flows through all aspects of the project; this is easily captured by the mantra "trust no one!" Now this may come across as negative, cynical and even untrustworthy - perhaps! But when you remind yourself what is at stake, and the risk that you, as the developer, are holding, we feel this is a realistic and prudent approach.

The construction phase is going to be the largest part of a development project and so the diligence on planning this aspect must be meticulous. This rests on two elements - firstly, the relationship that's built with your principal contractor and the trust and respect you have for each other; and secondly, the formal agreement you come to which details every aspect of the build - from the first materials purchased all the way through to the very end of the defect period, long after the buyers have moved in.

Most developers use a Joint Contract Tribunal, or JCT - essentially a legally binding contract that states what you, as the developer, must do, and what the principal contractor must do. There are various levels of JCT based on the size of the project, but importantly there is no project that is too small for a JCT, despite how overwhelming the size (and cost) of the document might initially seem. Don't cut corners here! Frequently during our development project we came across times where the easy option would have been to not do something, or choose the cheaper option. Here the saying "pay cheap, pay twice" could not be more appropriate (and believe us, we did!) so, a detailed contract is an absolute must!!

The future

Going forward we are continuing to build our portfolio through a mixture of commercial and residential development projects. What remains essential for us is ensuring we go into the right deal, which is only possible through laser sharp due diligence.

Property has opened up a world of opportunity which has allowed me to retire from the military after 21 years and given me a passion and fervour for entrepreneurism. Aside from property, we are also helping other business entrepreneurs adopt a military mindset to find their edge and power up their own businesses!

To conclude, the great thing about the property industry is the fantastic and inspirational people you meet every day, and the doors that naturally open through the connections you make - after all, who would have thought a snowboard trip to Courchevel could also be a business trip!?

TRANSFORMING SPACES: THE JOURNEY OF VICTORIA HOUSE FROM COMMERCIAL TO RESIDENTIAL
– PRAVEEN KARADIGUDDI & SUMIT AGARWAL

"The only way to do great work is to love what you do"
– Steve Jobs

Our partnership in the realm of commercial conversion is not just a business arrangement; it's a fusion of diverse experiences and a shared vision for transformative property development. I, Praveen Karadiguddi, bring to the table a robust background in digital consultancy and a keen interest in property development, fuelled by successful ventures in HMOs and multi-lets. My journey into commercial conversion was sparked by my eagerness to expand my portfolio, driven further by the invaluable mentorship of industry experts Nigel and Mark.

Sumit Agarwal, my partner, is the dynamic founder and managing partner of the DNS Group. An accountant by profession, Sumit's journey in the property world is marked by a substantial portfolio worth over £30 million. His expertise in financial management and strategic investment has been pivotal in our endeavours. Despite his success, Sumit was drawn to the untapped potential of commercial conversion, seeking to blend his financial acumen with innovative property development.

Our paths converged at a point where our visions aligned perfectly - transforming unused commercial spaces into vibrant residential communities. This shared ambition was not just about financial gain; it was about creating value, reviving spaces and contributing to the community. Our complementary skills – Sumit's financial expertise and my experience in growth and digital strategy – created a powerful synergy, enabling us to approach commercial conversion with a unique perspective.

The decision to embark on this journey was influenced by various factors. For Sumit, it was about diversifying his portfolio and exploring new avenues in property development. For me, it was an opportunity to apply my skills in a new domain, driven by the confidence gained from mentorship and previous successes in property investments.

Together, we stepped into the world of commercial conversion, equipped with a blend of expertise, a shared vision and a commitment to excellence. Our first project, the transformation of Victoria House, was not just a business venture - it was a manifestation of our combined aspirations and a stepping stone towards redefining urban living spaces.

Victoria House, High Wycombe was an office, old and empty for a while. The owner was tired of the empty office and business utilities bills stacking up. We have now converted the office to 30 flats - 12* two-beds and 18 one-beds. This was found by an agent for us who we constantly kept in touch with, and he got this deal to us before it came out to the market. Importance is building trust with him and executing as promised - we did exchange within a week unconditionally and complete within six weeks.

The process began with an intensive planning phase, where every detail was meticulously thought out. We focused on creating a design that was not only aesthetically pleasing but also practical and sustainable. The old office spaces were reimagined into 30 stylish flats, comprising 12 two-bedroom and 18 one-bedroom units. Each flat was designed to maximize space, light and comfort, reflecting a modern lifestyle. Our team, a blend of experienced professionals and enthusiastic newcomers, worked tirelessly to ensure that the conversion was smooth and efficient. We faced challenges, of course, but these were met with creative solutions that only added to the project's charm. Whether it was navigating the intricacies of building regulations or adapting to unexpected structural discoveries, our team's flexibility and problem-solving skills were paramount. Big thanks to Nigel Greene and Mark Stokes for their constant help and guidance throughout the project.

During

After

Our focus throughout was not just on the physical transformation but also on the social value we were adding to the community. We were constantly mindful of our impact on the neighbourhood, striving to enhance the local community while minimizing disruptions.

"The only way to do great work is to love what you do" – Steve Jobs

The transformation of Victoria House was not just about the physical conversion of the building; it was a profound journey of personal growth for both Sumit and myself. Throughout the process, our confidence soared as we navigated complex negotiations, managed intricate construction details and made impactful decisions. Each challenge we overcame, from financial management to on-site problem-solving, which enriched our skills and sharpened our vision. The project honed our ability to see potential where others saw obstacles. We learned the art of balancing ambition with pragmatism, often finding innovative solutions to seemingly insurmountable problems. Our journey with Victoria House has been a catalyst for personal development, equipping us with a clearer vision for future projects and an enhanced set of skills to realize them.

The completion of Victoria House was a moment of unparalleled pride and passion for us. Transforming a dilapidated office building into a vibrant residential complex was not just a financial investment, it was a contribution to the community. The sense of accomplishment was magnified by the positive feedback from residents and local stakeholders. Financially, the project was a resounding success. We self-funded the development, purchasing the property for £2.7 million and incurring construction costs of £2.2 million. The Gross Development Value (GDV) of the project stood at an impressive £7 million, yielding over 40% Return on Investment (ROI). This financial success is a testament to our meticulous planning, effective cost management and strategic execution.

Our decision to retain and rent out the 30 units has proven financially astute, generating annual revenues exceeding £450,000. This approach not only provides a steady income stream but also aligns with our long-term investment strategy, adding significant value to our portfolio.

This project was a labour of love, and it demanded creativity and problem-solving skills, especially when faced with unique challenges in design and construction logistics. Our team's ability to navigate these hurdles swiftly and effectively was crucial to our success.

The conversion of commercial spaces to residential units is increasingly popular, and Victoria House is a prime example of this trend. However, this project was a learning curve for us in several ways:

- Space Management: The limited space for material storage presented significant challenges, especially considering security concerns. Just-in-time ordering became a crucial strategy.

- Consultant Selection: The delays in design delivery highlighted the importance of choosing proactive consultants.

Final construction drawings must be ready before commencement to avoid project delays.

- Utility Management: Direct management of utilities, despite having M&E consultants, was a critical lesson. Regular follow-ups with utility companies are essential.

- Efficient Planning: The project's initial delay, due to design revisions, emphasized the need for efficient and thorough planning. Every decision impacts the timeline and budget.

- Budgeting Challenges: Perhaps one of the most significant lessons was in budget management. Our project budget exceeded initial estimates by 35% - a stark reminder of the importance of contingency planning and realistic budgeting in construction projects.

- Collaboration is Key: The success of Victoria House was a result of seamless collaboration among all stakeholders. This collaborative culture is vital for ensuring safety, functionality and aesthetic appeal.

The transformation of Victoria House has been a journey of learning, growth and collaboration. It stands as a testament to what can be achieved with passion, expertise and commitment, despite the challenges faced.

Next steps between us we have five more projects in the pipeline with over 25m of GDV.

MY JOURNEY TO CREATING MULTIGENERATIONAL WEALTH – MATT KAVANAGH

"If you want momentum, you'll have to create it yourself, right now, by getting up and getting started" - Ryan Holiday

In 2015 I was a commercial Finance Broker working near Blackfriars in the City of London. Even though I enjoyed my job, it wasn't something that I could see myself doing for the rest of my career. I had always been involved in property since leaving university, having worked as a letting agent and residential mortgage broker previously.

I had always wanted to get into property for myself and being newly married, and expecting our first child, I wanted a better life with more freedom. This really hit home when my son was born in March 2016. I was back to work after two weeks (which I had to take as holiday). In general, I saw him for half an hour in the morning before I went to work, and then half an hour in the evening before he went to bed. Yes, we had the weekends and I know that our experience is not unusual, but I felt that we could find a way to create much more quality time together as a family. Freedom was what I craved.

Having done some property training and education my father (Ian) and I started our property journey by buying up dilapidated houses in Corby, Northamptonshire and turning them into HMOs. We bought, added value, and then refinanced the houses to get most of our money back out. It was very much a 'cookie cutter' model, 4-bedroom houses converted into 6-bedroom HMOs. This gave us good income and the formula was working, but eventually, after 12 HMO conversions, as with many investors, we ran out of money to keep buying.

This is when we first started to think about a larger development project which could create either large capital sums, which we could use to reinvest, or further build the income we wanted, but in easier to manage large projects where you get the benefit of economies of scale.

I can sit here now, a little further down the road and say "getting into property" is the best decision I've ever made. Aside from the financial freedom, which we have managed to achieve, there has been a huge difference in the amount of time I have to spend with our now three children. The flexibility to go and watch our eldest as he starts to play school sports fixtures, or even just to make sure that I am either doing drop off or pick up every day, is an incredible privilege. I quit my job in London in 2018 and haven't looked back since. It's not always easy - being self-employed comes with its own pressures, but the freedom of choice makes it worth it.

When I look back, we were extremely lucky to get 'St Johns Terrace', the project I will talk about in my chapter. I had first seen the property on Rightmove, taken one look at the price, done a quick calculation based on square footage for build cost, and decided it wasn't going to work. I didn't even want to view it or spend any more time, they wanted too much money; it wasn't a deal.

A week later I got a call from the agent, someone we had a decent relationship with; he wanted us to come and take a look. I said I had seen in online and it wasn't going to work for us. Two more weeks went by and the agent phoned again - he really wanted us to see it, he was convinced that it would work and we should see it. I finally agreed and went to see the building in November 2019. The building was laid out perfectly for conversion, it was an office block which was built in the mid-nineties, windows were good, the structure was sound and there were no walls to remove. In theory, it was the easiest of conversions. We followed up our first viewing with another two days later with our builder. He confirmed our thinking and gave us some rough numbers for the conversion cost.

Our initial numbers looked like this:

GDV - £1,800,000

Build Costs - £350,000

Purchase Price – £950,000

Finance - £50,000

Profit - £450,000

Another big attraction to the project was the flexibility it could give us on the exit. Once converted we would be left with 9 two-bedroom apartments. These could be sold, rented out on ASTs for around £1,000 per month (£108,000 per annum), or they could be rented out as serviced accommodation. If we achieved 60% occupancy as SA then we could increase the income to closer to £200,000 per annum.

As some of you may have noticed from the dates above we ended up completing the deal during the covid pandemic in November 2020. This was the first, but not last challenge for the project and it immediately hit our timetable for the build. We had planned to throw a larger team at the project to get it completed quickly - this now went out of the window. While

we were able to continue with the conversion, we needed to keep the various trades and contractors separate and keep the number of people on site down, to make sure it was safe for everybody. We had a number of weeks with no progress, when contractors caught covid, and had to isolate for two weeks.

The conversion fell behind schedule even further due to delays in getting the utilities connected - with the benefit of hindsight, we would have started that process earlier and in future projects it has always been towards to the top of my list. Towards the end of the build we also started to see the large increases in the costs of materials which pushed the costs out beyond where we had initially thought. The added timescales also led to higher borrowing costs.

We funded the project through a high-net-worth JV partner - he was able to fund the purchase and build cost and the ownership was split 50/50. We have often preferred to fund our projects with private capital rather than bank funding, as it saves on fees and is usually more flexible if anything unexpected comes up. In this particular case it was critical as we had decided to retain the properties and rent them out as Serviced Accommodation. This meant we needed a lending partner than was committed to the long-term project and not just to see us through the build.

We handed over the keys to the apartments to our SA manager at the end of 2021. The apartments were all furnished nicely, with input and help from our SA managers and refurbished to a great standard. There is always a great pride in handing over the keys to a finished project ready for the next phase and in seeing the full transformation. As I am not from a building background my role is to support the build team and isn't based on site every day which makes the transformation often starker.

The site also taught us that the skills we acquired doing small HMO conversions still applied at this level, even though everything was supersized. The main difference was understanding how far the build timeframes can move on a longer project. On smaller projects we were looking at being in and out in six-eight weeks on average – projects on this scale take time, usually more than you think. The upside to the scale of it was that we were now producing around £15,000 a month of income instead of the £2,500 which was an average for our smaller HMOs.

The final figures for the project ended up as follows:

GDV - £1,800,000

Build Costs - £425,000

Purchase Price – £950,000

Finance £75,000

Profit - £350,000

Although the build costs had increased significantly for the project, we still managed our way through the process and came out with an excellent level of equity in the deal, as well as the cash flow mentioned above. We also hope to add to the value of the property as a whole by securing a commercial valuation based on the income being produced. This is a longer process as we need to show accounts for the first one-two years of SA income to support this. Assuming things stay strong on the SA side, we could push through £2m as a value.

The major learnings from the project were as follows:

1. Experience and education make projects like this ten times easier to make work. If you don't have any, then make sure you get the support around you in the right areas. You don't need to know all the answers, but you need people in your team that do.

2. Choosing the right partners is crucial. Things don't always go to plan during developments so it is vital to work with people that you can ride out the storms with, when they do arrive.

3. Multiple exits are a welcome choice when at the end of a project. Our primary focus, when we're looking at a project, is to make sure we have a number of routes to firstly get

investor money/loans paid back at the end, and secondly to make money from the project. Having multiple options give you greater flexibility and comfort if the market moves against you.

4. Every conversion deal is different. Unlike new build development where you can get to grips with a 'rule of thumb' build cost for your area, conversion is completely bespoke every time. There is no substitute for getting in for a viewing and seeing the required works for yourself.

Commercial conversions will certainly continue to be a big part of our plans for the future, the ability to take a disused or unloved building and transform it into much needed accommodation is a very satisfying process and there are huge opportunities for this type of project at the moment, and into the foreseeable future. With many high streets struggling up and down the country, there are chances to make an impact and renew some of these vacant spaces into town centre accommodation, which is greatly needed.

We also consider conversion projects over new build at the moment due to the timescales for planning applications to be decided. Councils all over the country are struggling with staffing and deciding applications on time. We have seen applications go from an average of three-four months for a decision to well over a year in many cases. There are no such issues with conversion of the existing building, assuming we are working with a prior approval.

Finally, we know from experience new build is getting harder to make work in many areas of the country. Build costs have increased greatly with a large proportion of this cost being in the ground with foundations. Unlike new build, conversion projects are viable across the whole country. For all these reasons, commercial conversions are top of our list for 2024. We will continue to retain assets when we can, although we don't shy away from taking on projects to sell, depending on how the market is treating us at the time.

MAKE OPPORTUNITY COUNT – DAVID KEMP AND MICHAEL MCQUADE

"Time kills a deal"

Reinvigorating seaside towns

Many of our high streets in towns and cities in the UK have encountered pressure from the changing ways in which we now shop, with more shopping taking place online, and less footfall and potential custom in more peripheral town centre locations. Seaside and other tourist-dependent locations have been especially hit, particularly due to successive lock-downs over the pandemic.

This has created the opportunity to reinvigorate tired and underused shops. Many of these shops have very deep ground floor space or upper floors that are connected to the shop via internal access and are therefore ideal for conversion.

In October 2021 Aspen Planning and DRK Planning started working together on the conversion of a part-three storey and part four-storey building in High Street, Margate.

The building is located in the town centre and in a conservation area. The frontage faces on to the High Street, but the rear elevation backs on to a narrow alleyway, Albert Terrace:

The rear of the building, as shown high windows and high brick wall, was more contemporary in appearance than the neighbouring buildings. Several of the neighbouring buildings in Albert Terrace, facing the back of the site, are Grade II listed.

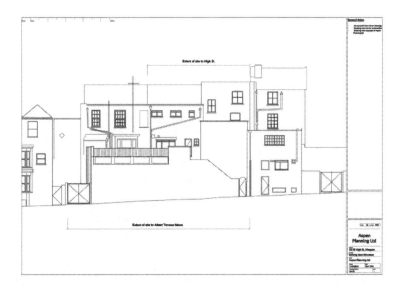

Purchase background

The vacant building was purchased in June 2021 after being found on Rightmove Commercial.

The previous commercial tenant was a national retailer that had gone into administration and the landlord/owner unexpectedly found themselves with a large empty building of 8,240 sqft that represented a liability to them in terms of security and also business rates. The previous owner was a commercial investor so the building was of no use to them, without a tenant, and they did not have the appetite to find a new commercial tenant in an ever-changing commercial market, nor to spend the time and money in re-purposing the building.

Surprisingly, the building did not have an immediate appeal to the developer market, and so had been on the market for a while and subject to a number of reductions in the asking price.

It was of a size and layout that required some comprehensive thinking on how to maximise a re-configuration of the existing space and this seemed to put most others off, who only took a cursory look at the potential for a quick win. This resulted in the building being purchased after a period of negotiation, that resulted in a purchase price at a level below the reduced advertising price.

In addition, there were various Landlord & Tenant legal issues to be resolved around the previous commercial tenant's lease as they had gone into administration before expiry of their lease. This was addressed by suggesting a delayed completion whereby the seller was given certainty by exchanging quickly with a long stop completion date to allow time for the seller to sort out the loose ends under the Landlord & Tenant Act 1954 so that the building was purchased free of legacy occupancy issues that could cause problems for the re-development and re-sale of the building.

Title splitting the building and access

We started designing the proposed scheme with the architect and the client 'with the end in mind' before working out how to get there through planning.

The building lent itself to a potential title split between front and rear parts. The front part comprised the retained shop floor space and two flats, with access from the High Street. It should be noted that part of the first and second floor comprised an existing flat over first and second floor to No.76 at the front. This is shown on the plans as greyed-out, so it is clear to officers that it is not part of the proposals; if this is included by mistake then officers could refuse the whole application on the basis that it includes space which is not in Class E (Commercial) Use.

The rear part would be accessed from the rear, via Albert Terrace, and would comprise six flats at ground and lower ground floors. The lower ground to the rear comprised storage and delivery space ancillary to the retail unit to the front, but the fall in the land to the rear created an opportunity to create new studio units at street level on to Albert Terrace. An existing rear access also provided means of access for bicycle and bin storage.

In approaching this project on this basis, it then became very clear as to where window or door positions would need to be altered in order to achieve good access and good natural light through the building and in each unit. These changes were addressed first through an application for planning permission.

The impact of the Conservation Area

The fact that the property is in a conservation area had two consequences. Firstly, it is important that the right person is instructed who has the experience, training and precision in drafting to meet these expectations. Well-presented plans will inspire confidence in Conservation and Planning officers. Poorly presented plans can undermine the prospect of consent.

Secondly, it is often the case in town centres, market towns and high street locations in conservation areas, that the presence of active retail frontage and sustainable retail uses contribute positively to the character of the conservation area. The loss of these units, either through proposing to replace the retail floor space completely, or by leaving an unviable retail unit that is too small or the wrong shape, can lead to a valid objection by the Council to an application for prior approval under Class MA in conservation areas.

Therefore, in conservation areas, before confirming the amount of floor space to the rear of shops that have the potential for conversion, it is not only the need to provide at least 37 sqm of space that needs to be checked (the minimum for a studio unit), but also the minimum shop area that could viably be retained and relet. This would need to be confirmed with local commercial agents, who should ideally be asked to provide a letter in support of the application to confirm that the proposed reduced unit is viable, with examples of enquiries or deals for similar sized units in the area to support their opinion.

Financial contributions to the Council

This scheme required the delivery of Section 106 undertakings to the Council. In this case, these involved the promise of financial payments towards Sites of Alternative Natural Greenspace (SANG) and the Strategic Access, Management and Monitoring (SAMM) contribution that goes with it. The exact amount was only about £2,000 in total but will vary from one local authority to another. Any sites or areas close to protected or natural habitats, such as upland, moorland, beaches, wetlands or woodlands might have such schemes linked to them; this is typical especially in parts of the south and south east of England. This should be checked from the outset with the local authority, who will also advise of the set tariff rates.

Such agreements will normally need to be signed by not only the owner of the land, but by lenders with a charge over the property. Some lenders might be unsure of or object to such documents, so enquiries with the lender must be made early, otherwise this can block the issue of prior approval if they withhold their consent to a s106 undertaking.

An opportunity to add value

As can be seen from the aerial shot shown below, this site presented a great opportunity to look to increase the building height.

Firstly, the roof heights along the High Street, as well as the building styles and finishes, are very varied. In particular, the building height to the left of the site is already one full storey higher and other buildings in the vicinity are also higher.

Secondly, the site already has a pitched roof, which due to its shallow pitch and the narrow width of the roadway to High Street, meant that this cannot be clearly seen from the ground level up.

As the building is clearly pre-1948 and located in a conservation area, permitted development rights for upwards only extensions are not available in this case, and so an application for full planning permission was made instead.

Applying for an extra storey therefore seemed like a 'natural' progression for the development in this case and made sense

in townscape and urban design terms. This would take the building to a total of four storeys – five storeys at the rear including the lower ground floor due to the fall in the street level to the rear. There was no precedent nearby for more storeys than this.

Issues and timescales

The extra storey application was submitted in mid-June, about a month after obtaining consent for change of use under Class MA. This time was taken up by application preparation – such as plans and drawings, preparation of the planning statement and application preparation.

After some delay, the permission was granted in late September 2022, about three months later. These delays were partly due to the unusual layout of the title in the land, in respect of which there was a 'flying freehold' (part of the upper floors within our ownership over sailed the lower floors to the neighbouring property in the terrace) and questions were raised by third parties regarding the legal interest in the rear access and courtyard to the site (where bin storage was proposed). These issues affected whether the application had been properly advertised by the Council, who were minded to restart the 3-week public consultation period as they were concerned that it had not been properly advertised to neighbours. Legal proof of title managed to avoid this.

The following table summarises the main stages and timescales:

STAGE	DATE SUBMITTED	DATE GRANTED	DURATION
Alterations to windows	23.11.2021	28.01.2022	2 months
Class MA: Ground floor (6 flats)	01.02.2022	03.05.2022	3 months
Class MA: 1st and 2nd floor (2 flats)	01.02.2022	03.05.2022	3 months
Additional floor (1 x 2-bed flat)	15.06.2022	29.09.2022	3 months

Opportunities and exit strategies

The main opportunity with this building was to increase the '£/sqft' value by obtaining change of use to residential for as much of the building as possible.

This was achieved through the various planning applications mentioned earlier and resulted in the re-purposing of over 5,000sqft of underutilised commercial space into residential usage comprising nine new flats with a remaining double fronted retail unit on the High Street.

The property offered multiple exit routes (once change of use was obtained) which can be grouped under three main headings and summarised as follows:

1. Develop out the residential elements and hold or sell as:

- Serviced Accommodation.

- BTL flats

- First time buyer flats.

- A HMO scheme (subject to amended layouts).

2. Separate onto different titles and sell as individual development opportunities for others to build-out:

- Title Split 1 - Rear part of the building comprising six flats which had a separate entrance at the rear of the building, off the corner of a nice period square serving the front of some listed buildings on the seafront. This could be sold as a standalone residential site and would attract a higher sales value independently as it didn't have any commercial elements that restrict the end values of residential units in a mixed-use building scenario.

- Title Split 2 – Front part of the building comprising the re-sized ground and lower ground floor retail unit and three flats on the upper floors.

- Title Split 3 – Separate the re-sized commercial unit from the upper floors and sell the retail unit to a commercial investor and the upper floors to a residential led developer.

3. Re-sized commercial unit:

- Rental Income - keep the commercial unit for rental income as part of annual earnings.

- Re-sale – tenant the unit on lease terms that give the maximum chance of yield compression to increase the capital value of the unit.

- Wealth Creation – keep and move the title for the commercial unit into a SSAS pension as part of tax efficient wealth building for the future.

- Subdivide - split the unit further from a double fronted unit to two single units for a higher rental yield per sqft.

Before committing to any of the above, the building was advertised for sale as a single development opportunity with the benefit of all the changes that had been approved through the various planning applications. This resulted in a sale being agreed to a local developer who develops to hold.

The selling price gave a return on total costs that exceeded our ROI criteria without the need to incur further costs in subdividing the building to sell the component parts separately. The annualised return was also better in selling at this stage and we eliminated the time risk involved in undertaking works and selling each part separately; there were no guarantees on how quickly a buyer could be found for each component part, or if indeed all parts would sell at a future date, which would be influenced by market conditions at that point in time.

Conclusions

Recent forecasts for the UK economy in the short to medium term will create an opportunity for developers and investors bold enough to capitalise on current landlord anxiety over the state of the commercial lettings market, especially in secondary or tertiary pitches, which may see already weak consumer demand drop-off even further as household budgets experience a greater squeeze.

These opportunities will be tailor-made for PD-led strategies, particularly making use of the new Class MA permitted development rights and, in the right circumstances on appropriate sites, offer further opportunity to add value at roof level with the right due diligence and an experienced professional team.

The planning process will continue to throw up challenges, especially given officer workloads and delays in managing applications, as well as the 'remoteness' of some officers. However, with mitigating strategies, persistence and good design, this can help protect and enhance the value of a scheme and ensure a tidy and viable exit from projects during this turbulent time.

Larger commercial buildings often offer much more opportunity to create a substantial uplift in value through change of use. That said, it requires a considered and comprehensive approach to properly analyse the available space in larger buildings and to fully identify and appraise all the positive and negative factors. This is crucial to be able to properly identify the various re-purposing options which, through continued and iterative further analysis, will show the optimum re-purposing option(s) to be pursued and the right order in which to undertake multiple planning applications.

Also, it is imperative to have identified clear goals at the outset of not only each development project but also before embarking on a career in property or change in direction from one type of development to another. A good degree of flexibility and agility is also very important so you can readily adjust or pivot as necessary along the way as new information comes available during the project cycle.

Numbers are also crucial in development and always need to be properly identified, understood and analysed constantly during the project; there is a real risk that an absence of this continuous focus on numbers results in decisions being made that may actually lead to seemingly more exciting things to talk about with others but which don't improve the bottom line and could, in fact, be detracting from it; also more money isn't necessarily better if it's spread over a longer period so annualized return is an important metric in any decision making process.

TRANSITIONING FROM THE WORLD OF CORPORATE TO PROPERTY DEVELOPMENT – JAY LALL

"You must take personal responsibility. You cannot change the circumstances, the seasons, or the wind, but you can change yourself. That is something you have charge of" - Jim Rohn

Introduction

Welcome to my property development journey.

I previously held a position in the corporate world as an IT Infrastructure Architect/Manager across various industries (pharmaceuticals, media and finance). This was a career I very much enjoyed over 21 years predominantly within the new data centre space. It was challenging and fulfilling, but at the same time the learnings and experiences were invaluable. I was fortunate enough to meet work colleagues who helped shape me both on a professional and personal level, and who I can still regard as friends today.

I began my property journey in 2003 investing in BTL property. The BTL portfolio was built up over time whilst working in the corporate world. During this time, I also invested with other property developers on their projects. This was mainly part of a lend and learn approach to gain early insights into the world of property development.

When my son was born I felt a seed was planted within me. I can only describe it as a seed of legacy. Although I knew I was continuing to enjoy my corporate career I wanted something more for my family, and to drive my newfound passion. Spending more quality time with family was also very important to me, especially since my second child was born. My father's work in the building trade, along with helping him on jobs in my younger years, spurred a passion for building.

This passion allowed me to make the jump and transition into the world of property development in 2021.

Set the scene of the development

My first development was located in Rochester, Kent. It was a commercial block located in a secondary retail/office parade surrounded by residential housing, and only a five-minute walk from the town centre. The property was able to be converted under Permitted Development (Prior Approval) which gave a level of certainty for the entire project.

The demand for commercial tenants on this particular parade was low over the previous years and some units were simply left empty, hence the block was a good candidate for conversion to residential. It is now a block of three flats with a high-quality specification.

The property was purchased at an auction. This was the first ever auction I attended, and I was fortunate enough to be in a position to secure the property within the required price bracket. There was a time challenge to ensure the auction legal pack was comprehensively reviewed by my solicitor, prior to the auction date. Thankfully this was completed within the required timeframe to allow the necessary due diligence items to be completed.

The First Development Journey

I should firstly state I educated myself with the required knowledge and systems to allow my first property development project to be successful. This allowed me to be more confident and at the same time minimise the risks associated with development projects. I was very much eager to apply the knowledge and systems on a 'live' project.

One of the first challenging parts of the journey involved engaging with the utility companies. The property only had provision for one gas metre, one electric metre and one water metre and they serviced all floors within the property.

I had to engage with each of the utility providers to install new infrastructure feeds for each of the utilities. So essentially each self-contained flat now has its own electric, gas and water metre. The reason for the early engagement with the utility providers is due to the timeframe for their tasks to be completed (digging underground to install new feeds, arrange permits, road closures etc). Due to the impact of Covid-19, the timeframes were further extended and there were some reports of six - eight months, and even longer, just to complete the task of provisioning new utility services. If I were to engage the utility providers during the later stages of the project, I would risk having completed flats with no utility services. Essentially this would mean they are not officially classified as habitable accommodation. Fortunately, this phase of the project was completed within the required timeframe.

www.sustainomics.co.uk

It is worth noting I also assigned myself to carry out the project management function. This was working alongside the main contractor that was assigned to the project. The experience allowed me to gain further insights into the practical nature of property development and keep to the timeframes, initiating escalations as required.

As the project progressed I gained invaluable insights for each of the trades on the project. The project lifecycle involved the key trades (electricians, plumbers etc) to complete their first fix and second fix tasks. These were some examples of terminologies I had to understand to allow me to map out the entire lifecycle of the project. This was also key to ensuring I knew what was in-scope to allow the various teams to move forward with their project deliverables. When each of the deliverables were met, this allowed me to measure the performance and release payments to the main contractor during the various project tranches.

The journey from commercial to residential property development was not without its challenges, but with each stage and each challenge overcome, the transformation to high quality living accommodation became more tangible. The once-empty property was now a canvas filled with potential, and with every passing day, the vision in my mind was inching closer to reality.

Overall, the whole project was a success. There were challenges but no real surprises. There were occasions where I had to be involved with managing the various trades due to unforeseen circumstances during Covid. There were also occasions when I had to escalate with suppliers to ensure building materials arrived on time during the various stages of the project.

Throughout the project lifecycle, I was also engaging with the building control inspectors, and the warranty provider for the build. One would have thought they both have the same set of requirements to maintain building standards. This was not the case. I found the build warranty inspectors were more stringent with their requirements. This was mainly due to the fact that the build warranty underwriters will not issue a certificate of cover (or have exclusions within their cover) if their requirements were not met. An example included new installation of mechanical fixings of the roof ridge tiles even if the existing ridge tiles had no issues with its mortar fixings.

When the project concluded, I took a moment to reflect on the hurdles that were overcome to reach this point. From some minor issues with the planning application to financial intricacies, each obstacle had been a stepping stone, propelling the project to move forward. The path from commercial to residential development had some level of complexities, but it was precisely those challenges that made the project all the more rewarding.

I personally found there was no real substitute for me to obtain this level of experience unless I completed the project in the way that I had. It provided me with clarity and confidence that property development is something I can pursue in place of my career in the corporate world.

Project Financials

Purchased - £290,000

Costs (inclusive of build costs, professional fees etc) - £121,000

GDV - £540,000

Funded via my SSAS (as a loanback) and private finance.

Project Exit

The property was retained under my holding company and now forms part of the rental portfolio. The title was split so now each flat has its own leasehold title. The Freehold has also been retained.

At the end of the project, the property was refinanced with a mainstream lender. This allowed funds to be recycled so the next project in the development pipeline could be funded.

Future strategy

With the success of my first development, I was eager to secure the second development. At the time of writing the second development has already been purchased.

Phase one of this project involves a conversion to seven flats on the upper floors and retaining the ground floor as commercial.

Phase two of the project involves the creation of multi-storey flats. This is also located on the same plot within the same area.

The project is another jump in terms of scale. Due to the larger size of the development, it was more appropriate to joint venture with a partner to deliver this project.

The knowledge and systems required to deliver the larger project will predominantly remain the same, but there are additional tasks to consider. Those items include engaging with other professionals - examples include a light surveyor to understand if there would be any light impact on neighbouring properties, and a CGI specialist to visualise the end state of the development. This also helps as part of the planning approval process, and marketing. There is also a full planning application element to the project.

Creative development-build methodologies also need to be explored to ensure planning approval can be achieved. When exploring these methodologies, it also provides an opportunity to look at efficiencies and cost control during the lifecycle of the project.

DAWSON HOUSE
– MICHELLE LUCAS AND
JO BALSTON

"Self belief is probably the most critical factor in success"
- Sir Steve Redgrave

[Jo] It has always been my ambition to work with spaces and buildings which transitioned into a career in Interior Design. I'd been lucky enough to have spent an enjoyable twenty years working for large developers on multi million-pound architectural schemes. It was rewarding, for the most part, as many of the buildings were hospitals or schools which gave me the opportunity to create spaces that enhanced the well-being of those the building served. The idea that people thrive when they are in spaces that nurture them is something that I still very much believe in and strive for.

On the birth of my son, Harris, I started to feel frustrated with the amount of travelling I did in my job and found myself working long hours in the office. Harris was being looked after by everyone but me. I could see him growing up faster than I had imagined, and I started to really want to find another way of living my life, to create more time for my family. I'd become aware of a path less traditionally trodden, and I wanted to show my son too. I started taking myself to property network-ing events as a way to learn. I was pretty clear I wanted to get into development - I just had no idea how this would happen. It was at this point that several stars aligned!

I was invited to attend a year's mentorship program to learn about small scale property development. The course focused on three pillars: business, property development and mind-set. As someone who'd spend their career in a corporate world, the business and mindset aspects appealed to me. I decided this was the moment to leave my job behind and get stuck in.

Skip a couple of years, lots of knowledge and growth and throw a JV partner into the mix. Michelle and I were in the middle of buying not one, but two commercial buildings. I had met Michelle on our mentorship. We got to know each other over the year, and formed our partnership at the start of 2021. She knew I was holding back because I was a bit scared of the business and finances, both things she has experience and skill in. While she found imagining a building and seeing the potential in something a bit tired and old really challenging, this is something I love; we also share very similar values around family and creating time freedom. Hence our partnership has worked out well.

[Michelle] I was looking for a career path that would allow me to spend time with my daughter Brooke. I had spent the first 10 years of her life, and many years prior, working long hours in the hospitality industry. Whilst I loved the pace of running my own businesses, it didn't fit with my future as a single parent.

After selling my business I used the proceeds to purchase a small run-down property to refurbish; not long after I came across a training company that led me to see other property strategies. I knew then I wanted to learn more about development. Getting to know Jo on the mentorship program I began to understand that my weaknesses could be overcome with a good business partner who could take reigns on the areas I felt less confident in - because we have different strengths and experience, we work well together.

The project we launched our business with became known as Dawson House and is in the heart of Southampton City

Centre, just a short walk from the main shopping area and station. While a very busy urban setting, it is directly opposite a leafy green which provides a pleasing vista from the front of the building. It started off as two very tired Victorian office buildings, side by side on a little terrace. The older parts of the building, originally constructed in 1880, have spacious high ceilings and large sash windows. We bought both buildings, gained permission through permitted development to convert the use to residential, then applied for planning to add a rear mansard extension and they became eleven flats.

Originally, we found the first building on an estate agents' website. We knew there were changes coming to UK space standards - the size of a one-bed flat was increasing from 30m2 to 39m2 so we stacked our numbers based on a conservative view, and the new guidance. We offered our price, but we were told our offer 'wasn't compelling enough'.

Not long after, the agent rang to tell us that the building next door was about to go on the market, and asked if we would be interested. The next door property was very similar in many ways, although slightly less up together and less extended at the rear. It had the additional challenge of a commercial tenant. Our offer was subject to a delayed completion because we required vacant possession. This time our offer was accepted and we were off the starting blocks.

We started work with our architect so he could submit our permitted development application. In the meantime, Michelle was speaking to the Agent regularly to check the progress of the sale going on next door. Eventually our perseverance and regular chats paid off - he told her that the sale

on the original building had fallen through! She immediately reinstated our original offer and rang me to tell me she'd bought another building!!

We each put in our own funds towards professional fees. The offices were purchased predominantly with private investor loans, from long term friends of Michelle's. She had introduced them to the benefits of owning and administering their own SSAS (Small Self-Administered Scheme) Pension and, in turn, we became their first investment. The security we gave was a second charge over the buildings. The construction and remaining professional fees came via our broker, from a lending company, who had a first charge over the buildings. Both our private investors and our bank became integral to the team. We made sure we gave monthly progress updates and regular site visits throughout the project so our investors knew what was happening, could get their hands dirty, don a site hat and see how things were going first hand.

Achieving planning was relatively smooth sailing. The permitted development applications went through, without any issues, giving us permission to change the two buildings into ten one-bed flats. We then applied for permission to create a new two-bedroomed flat on the back of the building by way of a mansard extension that spanned across the rear of both buildings. We also applied to add a new porch extension on the front as this helped to unify the appearance of the two buildings at ground level. One building was in more of its original form, but the other had a large glass shop front. Given its proximity to the road, the window didn't offer any privacy, once the space was converted, which was something we addressed with the new proposal.

We had a full team working with us on the project - architect, structural engineer, project manager and cost consultant. The works were put out to tender by our project manager and a main contractor was secured on an Intermediate JCT Contract. We embarked on stripping out the building in December 2021. Full works began in January 2022.

Generally, the building works went well, albeit they took longer than planned. The final product looked fantastic, with spaces that felt light, airy and modern, and appealed to both investors and first-time buyers. There were, of course, challenges getting to the end, as anyone would expect there to be, and we had our fair share. Thanks to our determination to find solutions and with the help of the team, we got through them.

Early in the build, as with any project where you are stripping away old layers, we had some structural surprises. The building was taken completely back to brick and was being reconfigured quite heavily, creating new structural openings and removing one of the main staircases to enlarge the available floor area. A large crack was discovered, stretching from the ground floor to the roof, which was slightly alarming. It had been hiding under layers of old lath and plaster so would never have been found on the structural survey. After some studying and head scratching amongst the team, it was deemed a historic crack and was soon rectified by 'stitching' the masonry back together.

We marketed the flats off plan using CGI images and had a number of sales lined up waiting for the building to complete. Some of the sales fell through when the construction works overran, and although we did eventually sell all the units, it took a little longer than we were expecting.

We always planned to sell the flats as our primary exit as Dawson House was our first project. We wanted to experience all aspects of the process from start to finish and test working together. Our secondary exit was to keep the flats for our portfolio and rent them. Regardless of the exit, the most important thing to us was always to repay our investors. Our second charge lenders have earned more interest than originally proposed, as it took slightly longer to replay them.

One of the most rewarding aspects of the renovation of Dawson House has been seeing such tired, old buildings come back to life again. The people living there have created a lovely little community and it feels like a welcoming place to live. Now the dust has settled, it's a fantastic feeling to reflect on what we achieved. We are really proud of Dawson House. We are also ready for the next challenge and growth of our business. We have been going through a process of refining our approach, going forward, and are looking for more similar projects to get our teeth into alongside building our investor network. This time, rather than primarily planning to sell the units, we would like to have options to grow our cash flow as well.

[Jo] This project has been a huge learning experience in every way. There are the obvious learning curves around running a construction project, but as I had always been an employee, I've also had to learn how to run a business. I've been grateful

to have partnered with someone who has years of business experience. There are more personal growth shifts as well, which are inevitable when embarking on something new, such as learning how to manage stress, digging deep and finding resilience when things feel challenging. It's also important to remember to enjoy the journey we're on and celebrate the wins - no matter how small.

I have learned the importance of building strong relationships, not only with our professional team and investors, but across everyone we have come in contact with. Michelle and I have had to discover how to work with each other, so we can support each other in whichever way is needed. And most importantly, maintaining discipline around working for yourself, managing time and keeping healthy boundaries so that business doesn't take over and encroach on family time.

[Michelle] It's important to make sure key conversations are documented so everyone is clear and all decisions are agreed. We experienced frustrating situations where things that had been discussed changed after being verbally decided.

Expect delays and changes along the journey and be prepared to change tack if something isn't working out as originally planned. Celebrate your wins along the way and don't dwell on anything negative - find the solution and move forward. The professional team is crucial. Don't be afraid to swap members within your team if someone is underperforming. Deal with it quickly so things don't escalate.

I think, for me, the training and mentorship along the way has been crucial for our success. It's a big responsibility delivering a building project with borrowed funds. Guard them with your life.

TURNING A VICTORIAN PUB INTO AN ENERGY EFFICIENT CO-LIVING HOME
– CATHY MOCKE

"I hear and I forget, I see and I remember,
I do and I understand"
Confucius (551-479 BCE)

I have had a lifetime in construction and been very fortunate to have had a varied and exciting career as an architect. Working largely in hospitality, I've been involved in projects on a global scale and lived and worked in Europe, the Middle East and in Asia. Looking towards a more balanced life, I started looking at how I could take more control of my personal wealth and create a secure future for myself, and my family, without being at the whim of an employer. In these fickle times I realised that I really needed to be more self-sufficient in that regard. That's when I started looking to invest in property, and my husband and I embarked on our development career, aided by the decision to set up our SSAS to help to fund our investments. We completed our first HMO in 2020, just before Covid, and were on the lookout for another project.

I had walked past the building many times, intrigued by the original 'Butchers Arms' sign etched into one of the down-

www.sustainomics.co.uk

stairs windows. It had clearly been abandoned with no sign of life, in an ideal location on the edge of the Town Centre, built as a pub in the 1880's but decommissioned in the mid 509s and been intermittently used as a residence since then.

I was delighted to see an auction sign go up early in 2020, during Covid lock down restrictions. We were successful at the

auction (actually, post auction, as it had failed to sell at the reserve price!) in September 2020. A strange situation as it was auctioned by a local auction house who were primarily selling off the contents, so not really on the radar of other property developers. We got lucky!

We bought it for cash, eventually completing in December 2020, scraping together our pennies and pounds, supplemented with a loan from a friend who had been an angel investor on our previous HMO project. We then looked for bridging to develop it but the valuer down valued it considerably, due to its state (although its over 200sq.m, double fronted, end of terrace they were comparing it with 50sq.m mid terrace 2 up/2 downs!). We then looked to development finance, hoping to raise enough funds to reimburse some of the purchase costs and fund the conversion. The lender and

their professional team of QS and valuer were incredibly pedantic and rigid in their approach. At the same time we were trying to get the title registered with land registry and all we had was several wax paper and velum title plans which needed to be pieced together, like a puzzle. This HMLR process was really dragging on and by the time we were in a position to move forward, the builder was no longer available, the valuation had to be re-done, another builder needed to be found - and this went on.

While all this delay was happening, I started looking at how we could improve the energy efficiency of the building. I have always been interested in environmental issues and sustainability and have always endeavoured to take this approach both as an architect, for my clients, and in our own developments. Given we needed to take the building back to brick, I had a strong feeling that this project could offer us a unique opportunity to go even further in implementing some serious energy saving strategies. I was particularly interested in air quality, and the potential for a balanced mechanical ventilation system to deal with pollution, acoustic and security issues for the tenants. The building sits at the edge of the pavement, near to some traffic lights on a busy town centre thoroughfare. Installing a balanced ventilation system would ensue both good air quality and improved security to the downstairs rooms, whose windows opened directly onto the pavement. I was familiar with the system, having worked on several large residential projects where this is included as standard. Little did I know that this idea would become the seed for the full-blown low energy retrofit strategy we ended up implementing. Whilst looking for an installer for the MVHR (mechanical ventilation with heat recovery) system, I met someone who was an expert in MVHR, renewables and a builder to boot.

Together we developed the scheme to reduce the energy demand by taking the 'fabric first' approach by reducing heat loss, then using renewables to power the building. This would reduce our overall energy costs and our carbon emissions. Although he'd been in the renewables industry for 20 years, he was on the cusp of starting his own business with a partner and was keen to use the project as a case study. We agreed a way forward that would benefit both of us.

I also realised no formal lender would allow us to take this 'partnership' approach and would insist on a standard JCT Contract and a builder with a long track record, in this type of project. The QS's estimates were way off the scale as well, insisting on adding in costs for consultants who weren't needed, £1200 per room for individual structural warranties (??), huge costs for new services connections we didn't need, etc, etc. We realised if we stayed with the lender, we'd need to raise even more additional funds and be subject to ongoing costs for the monitoring surveyor, and so on. Added to that, their anticipated exclusion of this partner to carry the project through construction - a dilemma!

At about the same time this was happening, our SSAS became fully funded and we were able to take a loan back for the development of the property. I reached out to the SSAS community and very quickly we attracted three very interested investors. They were keen to learn more about what we were doing and had their own personal interest in the sustainable approach to development. We said goodbye to the lender (and wrote off some substantial fees - ouch!) and took complete control of the whole process.

We planned to convert the building from C3 to C4 under permitted development so there were no planning issues.

We dealt with the thermal envelope first to reduce heat loss and heating demand. The leaky roof was stripped back, repaired, insulated and re-laid. We used solar reflective breathable roofing felt to control solar heat gain. In a well-insulated building overheating can actually become an issue so we needed to take steps to mitigate that as well. The solar panels (16 units x 400 watts each) were laid on flashing trays directly on the roof battens, saving on expensive slate roof tiles with the added aesthetic advantage of being a flush system.

External windows and doors were all replaced with thermally efficient, but readily available, units. The external walls were insulated internally and dry-lined. The entire wall and roof installation was made airtight, ensuring continuity of the airtightness through attention to detail, particularly where floors meet walls and around windows and doors. Airtightness tape and sealant was installed around any penetrations and interfaces between walls and windows and doors, rooflights, etc. The floors were largely ground bearing slab with a small cellar under one room. These were insulated by laying insulation over the floor and laying finishes on top of that. The cellar soffit and external walls were also insulated.

The project was thermally modelled using Passivhaus software called a PHPP to calculate energy usage and heat loss.

We also completed very detailed calculations for the U-values of the thermal envelope. The modelling estimated a total heating demand to be 1.1kW, the same as is provided by a standard medium sized radiator - for a 210sq.m building!

As mentioned earlier, the MVHR system is key to controlling heat loss and reducing heat demand. This allows fresh air to be pumped into the building without having to open the windows for fresh air, dealing with air quality, acoustic and security issues in the process. The system draws in fresh air from

www.sustainomics.co.uk

the outside and distributes it into the bedrooms and living spaces, which is then extracted from the bathrooms and the kitchen through a heat exchanger (this is bypassed in the summer). The heat exchanger extracts the heat energy from the return air and then the unit purges the stale air. The incoming fresh air is filtered for pollen and pollutants and heated by this recovered heat energy. The air then passes over a coil, heated or cooled by the ASHP, should additional heating/cooling be required. The system provides an excellent level of air quality with a complete air change occurring every two hours. Essentially the MVHR conserves energy within the building and the occupants, appliances and activities contribute to the heating (internal heat gains) creating an effective heat source. Cooling mode is used in summer to maintain a steady 20 degrees within the building year-round.

Our primary heating load is now the hot water as space heating is negligible. We installed an 11kW heat pump externally which primarily heats the hot water within a 500Litre cylinder.

The solar PV system is connected to a battery for storage and a power diverter. When the battery is full, the diverter diverts power to the hot water tank. Instead of excess energy going back to the grid at minimal pay back to us, the solar was an extra over cost of around £8000 but will generate over 3100kW hours per annum. Given our total energy demand is calculated to be 5150kW, that's 60% of our energy needs. We are currently monitoring the monthly generation and it is all looking to be on target.

The building was transformed into a high quality, generously proportioned, six en-suite bedroom co-living house, with a large communal kitchen/living space, a separate TV snug and a utility room with a washer and heat pump dryer. So far the energy bills are in line with the modelling estimates. In March 2024, we will have recorded a full year's usage and be able to do an accurate review.

We have been fortunate to team up with a local, internationally renowned tailoring school which attracts students from all over the world, who have become our tenants. Our first cohort ranged in age from 24 to 69! The best thing is they treat the house as their home and really buy into the whole low energy thing. We hope that influences them to take the message back with them, to their various countries!

A full SAP based EPC (this is a detailed calculation based on actual data as opposed to the standard RdSAP which is a reduced method calculation) was commissioned, which resulted in an A rated Energy Performance Certificate (EPC). Only 0.1% of existing buildings in the UK have an A EPC, so we were thrilled all our hard work paid off. Not only does this represent the future savings in energy bills that we will benefit from, but it has also future-proofed and improved the intrinsic value of the property. A previous RICS Red Book valuation which was carried out by a surveyor appointed by the development finance lender based on a standard conversion, was £350k. When we came to re-finance, we received an uplifted valuation of £450k - this was approximately 18 months after the first valuation.

During the construction period, we held open days for anyone who was interested. This included developers, landlords, homeowners, etc. As well as showing them the installation, I developed a series of visual aids to explain the retrofit and the cumulative impact of the different measures on the energy use of the building. Many came to us in a state of confusion; where do we start? We hope that our open days and the information we were able to communicate helped to clarify what the important decisions are in the early stages of a project such as this. Another key factor was how to avoid unintended consequences, through making the wrong decisions. This information has also been encapsulated in an ever-evolving case study talk I have now done to several groups, including EquaAcademy.

We also received a local Civic Trust award for our low energy credentials from the local Civic Trust Society, of which we are extremely proud.

THE STORY OF A 19TH CENTURY GENTLEMEN'S CLUB RESTORED TO ITS FULL GLORY – RICHIKO OLRICHS

"Our life is what our thoughts make it" - Marcus Aurelius

Introduction

In the early years of my career, life was a constant juggling act. Between the demands of a 9-to-5 job and the pressing need for financial stability, I found myself yearning for a change. This chapter delves into the transformative journey I embarked upon, leveraging property development and commercial conversions to not only meet my personal and financial goals, but to thrive in the process.

Although I was fortunate to have a successful career of over 15 years in the aviation and hospitality industry, the daily grind left me feeling drained and unfulfilled. Time with my family was scarce, and financial worries loomed over me like a dark cloud. A turning point in my life came when the company I was working for went through a global restructure and hundreds of jobs were lost. It was a very stressful period in my life. I knew there had to be a better way to live and the world of property development seemed like a promising avenue for change.

Setting the Scene

I started my property development journey with several smaller projects, doing single let and HMO refurbishments. I had gained some good property development experience by doing these residential projects when I came across the opportunity of converting an old, neglected office in the heart of Hartlepool into residential apartments. It was a beautiful Victorian building dating from 1899 with immense potential.

Once a meeting place for the town's businessmen of the mid-20th Century, this building was most recently run as serviced office accommodation before the owner submitted plans for it to be converted into six apartments. The offices had been vacated for several years and the building had been empty. I envisioned it as a vibrant residential space that could breathe new life into the community.

Finding the Project

The project came to my attention via my project manager, who I had been successfully working with on previous residential projects, and it felt like fate had guided me to this opportunity. He had been assigned to this development as the project manager when he learned that the buyer had suddenly pulled out. He brought the project to me as he knew that if I were to purchase it, he could still project manage it. He put me in touch with the owner and the negotiation process started. We agreed on the purchase price, however, after we received the valuation report from the bank, we had to renegotiate my initial offer as the valuation came back lower than the offer price. A creative solution was needed to secure the deal, which involved an offer with an overage on the end GDV. The seller was happy with this, and we eventually sealed the deal to move forward with the purchase.

The Transformation

The conversion process was both challenging and invigorating. Despite the inevitable setbacks, I approached them as

learning experiences rather than obstacles. This chapter explores the process with an emphasis on inspiration, highlighting the triumphs and creative solutions that made the project a success.

The challenges started even before I owned the property. We waited for months before we finally obtained the final decision notice from the council regarding the planning permission, a crucial piece of paper without which we were unable to move forward with the legal purchase. It involved regular and open communication with all the stakeholders, including the council's planning department, the current owner, the architect, and my project manager who all had to provide input and information necessary to get the final decision over the line.

We also faced challenges with building regulations. As it's an old building, it was not an easy task to bring the apartments up to a modern standard compliant with building regulations. This included sound insulation and EPC. We were also limited by the fact that the building is in a conservation area which meant we were not able to make any changes to the existing windows and we were not allowed to install double glazing. The solution around this was to install laminated glass which met the certification standards and requirements of building control as well as improving the EPC. I was guided by my architect and project manager throughout this process, as I lacked the specific knowledge myself with regards to which materials were best fit for purpose to satisfy building regulations and deliver that high standard of quality.

Personal Development

Throughout the project, I evolved personally, gaining confidence, honing my skills and developing a clearer vision for my future in property development. It's incredible how this journey shaped not only the building, but also me. Every challenge

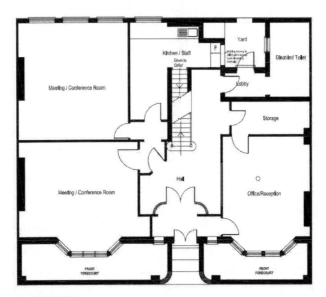

Meeting / Conference Room

Kitchen / Staff

Yard

Disabled Toilet

Down to Cellar

Lobby

Storage

Meeting / Conference Room

Hall

Office/Reception

FRONT FORECOURT

FRONT FORECOURT

SITE & GROUND FLOOR PLAN 1:50

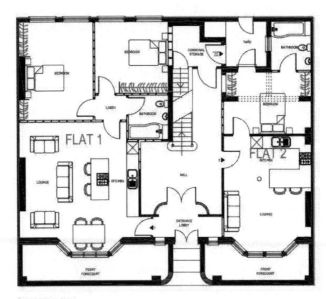

BEDROOM

COMMUNAL STORAGE

YARD

BATHROOM

BEDROOM

LOBBY

BATHROOM

BEDROOM

FLAT 1

FLAT 2

LOUNGE

KITCHEN

HALL

KITCHEN

LOUNGE

ENTRANCE LOBBY

FRONT FORECOURT

FRONT FORECOURT

SITE & GROUND FLOOR PLAN 1:50

faced provided an opportunity to learn and grow. We often needed to think on our feet and come up with solutions for the problems we encountered. Great teamwork was an essential element of making this project a success and it required me to be the best version of myself when it comes to people skills and communication. As there were so many new elements as part of this project, I was stretched beyond my comfort zone and there were times where I felt a lot of stress and pressure. As the developer, you are the one juggling all the balls to try and keep them all in the air. You are the one dealing with the lender, the monitoring surveyor, the architect, the council, project manager, interior designers, solicitors - and the list goes on. Ensuring that communication is flowing, and everyone is kept informed, is a key part of the developer's role. My previous experience in corporate life, managing large teams, certainly helped me throughout this process. There were times when I needed to dig deep and wasn't sure how to solve a particular problem. I benefited from having access to great mentors who could guide me with their experience, something I found invaluable and helped me grow even further throughout the process.

Financial Overview

The asking price for the building was £240,000. We initially agreed on a purchase price of £220,000 which we revised to £170,000 after we received the valuation report. We agreed an overage of £50,000, subject to the GDV. The total cost of the development was £225,000 which was fully funded by development finance. We purchased the building using a bridging loan at 50% LTV. The remainder of the funds came

from private capital from my business partner. The RICS Red Book valuation valued the finished product at £600,000.

The Exit

The story of the property's journey doesn't end with its transformation. I explored how I decided to conclude the conversion—whether by selling or holding the property—weighing the pros and cons of each option. My business partner and I decided that we would each retain two of the apartments and sell the remaining two to another investor, which meant we are not leaving any money in this deal. All apartments will be fully furnished and stylishly decorated, and they will be operated as serviced apartments for short term rentals. The expected annual turnover is £164,000, based on an average occupancy of 75%. We decided on this exit due to the central location of this property. It is in the middle of the town centre and a five-minute walk from the main train station. Around the corner from the property are the newly built Northern Studios, a large complex of over 3000 sqm of Hollywood style film and television production studios. The Studios have already expressed interest in the apartments, due to its proximity, as they are expecting regular visits from film and television crew from out of town who will need high quality accommodation.

Lessons Learned

In the spirit of inspiration, I share valuable lessons gleaned from this experience. These insights, although high-level, shed light on the importance of perseverance, adaptability, and the power of believing in one's vision. As I write this chapter, the project is in its early stages of development and there will be more lessons to come as we progress further towards completion.

A key insight for me is the importance of having a strong team around you. Property development is first and foremost about people. Working together with people, building great relationships, and solving problems together is a key element to success. People must feel comfortable working with you and it is essential that trust is built amongst the team. When the trust in each other is there, you can have disagreements or difficult conversations without jeopardizing the relationship.

Another key lesson for me was that I needed to have sufficient knowledge of the process to be able to make the right decisions for the project and for the business. This meant brushing up on my knowledge of project management, the planning process, development finance and building regulations as these were all issues that were new to me as I hadn't dealt with these in previous projects. It meant finding the right support around me including experienced mentors who helped guide me, professional contacts such as a planning consultant, tax advisor and specialist mortgage advisor - and the list goes on. Without this support and gaining further knowledge, I would have made some costly mistakes as a result.

Future Strategies

The chapter concludes with a glimpse into my future commercial conversion strategy and next steps. It's a testament to the enduring passion and commitment that this journey has ignited within me. There is something exciting and rewarding about restoring an old building back to its full glory so that it can play its part in the community again. The future strategy is to look for more of these types of projects, with the use of permitted development or planning permission to convert empty commercial buildings into residential properties.

This chapter serves as a beacon of hope for those seeking a path from adversity to achievement, illustrating how commercial to residential conversions can be a transformative journey on both personal and financial fronts.

SCALING UP – ALEX POTOCKI AND HELEN CLARKE

"Don't get so busy making a living that you forget to make a life..."
– Dolly Parton

It has to be said, I never really enjoyed being an employee. Although I've spent most of my career successfully building high performance teams across various industries from construction to retail, I've never found it easy to conform to a corporate 'cookie cutter' structure. There's always this thought in the back of your mind that you're building someone else's dream. On a practical level, I had too much of an entrepreneurial spirit and I always found it difficult to be restricted by the constraints that you often find in corporate business.

As a side hustle to my career, I have always renovated houses and been a landlord since 1998. Property has always looked after me and challenged me in all the right ways - budget control, specification choice and always keeping the end user and profit margin in mind. There has always been something very satisfying knowing that you are providing a really good quality home for someone, maybe even a whole family.

Back in January 2020, I started to take the time to consider what I really wanted out of life. It certainly wasn't 60 hour working weeks and the phone never stopping ringing! Redundancy gave me an amazing opportunity to reinvent myself and create the life I wanted. I signed up for a number of online property courses from four different training academies. By June 2020 I'd set up my first limited company, became my own boss, and set my own timetable and priorities. Property allowed me the freedom to do this.

Roll forward just over three years and we have nine projects completed and a mixed property portfolio of HMO's, BTL's and serviced accommodation. Our current project is a former 10-bedroom guest house over four storeys, situated right on the sea front in the North West coastal town of Morecambe. The property has been converted into three residential apartments – a second floor two-bedroom apartment, a first floor two-bedroom apartment and a three-bedroom maisonette across the ground floor and lower ground floor.

Nestled between Lancaster and the Lake District, Morecambe is a town on the brink of regeneration following the planning approval and government backed funding of Eden Project North. Our decisions to invest in this town over the next five years were largely driven by the confirmation of Eden and the potential of future proofing our investment. It's also true that both my partner (Helen) and I have a soft spot for this Victorian seaside town. In my previous career as a Property Director for Aldi, I secured and purchased the land of the Aldi store on the seafront, and Helen spent many of her days as a student at Lancaster University sampling the nightlife that Morecambe had to offer in the late 1990's!

We began our search for a commercial property in Morecambe in August 2022. We spent many weekends walking the streets to really understand the town, the local attractions and the potential on offer. We introduced ourselves to many local estate agents and attended numerous viewings across the town, which included former pubs, guest houses, hotels and large venue buildings. At the end of one Saturday afternoon, as we were heading home, we drove along the sea front and noticed a very good looking property that was showing on the agents website as 'sold subject to contract'.

We decided to call the agent and as luck would have it, they were unsure that the sale would proceed. We made an appointment to view the next weekend, and from that first initial viewing, we knew that this could become something very special. Plans had been drawn up by a local architect to convert the building into three apartments, but the application had not yet been submitted. The sale with the previous seller fell through within days of our viewing and suddenly the estate agent was chasing us on behalf of his very motivated seller. We were able to agree heads of terms on the property, with a significant discount, and the planning application was immediately submitted (and paid for) by the seller.

The purchase price for this property was £300K and our refurbishment budget was £160K. This was funded by £40K of our own funds and the remainder by our angel investor. The planned GDV was £680K and it was always our intention to keep and refinance the property, once work was complete. Given the location and the potential ripple-effect of Eden Project North on the horizon, the most profitable strategy is to operate them as serviced accommodation. Our end goal is to refinance each apartment onto its own mortgage, title split the building and then pay our investor back with the agreed interest.

The sale completed in February 2023, and we were up and running on our very first commercial conversion project! How exciting and totally nerve-racking all at the same time. This felt like a big step up to take from our previous projects, given there was a planning process to manage - we would need to bring in some new trades people to set up and working with an angel investor as part of a joint venture. Also, all of the numbers were bigger!

The strip out phase was more intense than we had anticipated, as most of the internal stud partition walls and lath and plaster ceilings needed to be replaced. We have two excellent labourers in our property power team (our best kept secret!) who've worked with us now on several projects. During the strip out phase they spent most of their days wearing white body suits, masks and protective glasses. It was like Crime Scene Investigation Morecambe! In addition to our labourers, we already had a number of trades secured to bring to the project; we've worked with our plasterers for 15 years, the electricians we have are family of close friends and our painter and decorator have also been working with us now for a couple of years. Securing a builder was the tricky part. We had two different local building companies lined up to do the job. Both agreed the scope of works, both gave their quotes - and both let us down.

Whenever we have a gap to fill in our property power team, one of our most effective ways to find new trades is to photograph work vans that we see out and about in the local area, and then give them a call. We spotted a local builder's van and did just that. This time we got lucky and secured, what has turned out to be, an excellent builder who we've developed a strong relationship with over the course of the last six months. His joiner has been on the job pretty much every day and has contributed to the overall success of the refurb project. A little tip for keeping your trades happy is to pay them at the end of each week for the work they have done. Not only do you keep them motivated, as they're never waiting for payment, it's also a great way to help you keep on track with your budgeting.

Overall, the project is just £6K over its original £160K refurb budget and a week ahead of its original planned programme of work. It takes a lot of work to bring in a project close to its budget, particularly where groundworks, roofing and replacing any of the services are involved. Experience has taught us that it pays to shop around for your materials – we have saved nearly £10K through negotiation, buying materials when there are deals on and by using loyalty cards.

We selected a high specification and the team have attained a high-quality finish. Valuations from local estate agents have exceeded our own estimations – our two-bedroom apartments have a suggested asking price of £250K and the three-bedroom maisonette is estimated to be worth north of £300K. This would result in a GDV of £800K so it makes the hard work and graft feel extremely worthwhile.

Seeing the project come to completion makes you feel both satisfied and proud. There's a great sense of achievement in taking a run-down property and turning it into something beautiful and into someone's home. As the saying goes, "the more you do, the better you get" - each project we've done seems smoother, better managed and has resulted in an end product that improves time after time.

When you see the look of amazement on the estate agents faces as you show them around your property, and you step back and say to yourself "wow, look at what we've created" – that's the moment right there. The moment that reminds you that this is your passion, this is exactly where you want to be and it's exactly what you want to be doing.

The project has been very enjoyable but also another great learning experience. One thing I'm getting better at is to remember my role as the client. In previous projects I tend to get involved in some of the tasks or fill in when I'm waiting for tradesmen to start on site. There's always the temptation, within a project, to roll your sleeves up and get stuck in, but I'm trying to keep this to a minimum. And as Helen often reminds me, "please will you leave the plumbing to the professionals!!"

Having a team you can trust is a crucial part of the overall project success. It also meant that I was able to take a three-week holiday in the USA, during the later stages of the project. Property gives you the freedom to enjoy your time as you want to take it, so with equal measures we work hard and take time out to live our lives too.

Our confidence and appetite for bigger commercial projects has certainly accelerated, and with the backing of an investor who knows, likes and trusts us – it feels more comfortable to take a greater step with each new project that we embark upon. We wouldn't have been able to do any of this without the education and re-training we received three years ago and the continual support of a business mentor who is ahead of you in expertise.

So what does the future hold? Well, I'm excited to say we've recently exchanged on a second commercial project in More-cambe. This one is just a little bit bigger – it's a former 44 bedroom hotel! Our plans are to build ten large residential apartments on the upper two floors, and an aparthotel on the lower three floors. There's also an opportunity to build six new houses on the huge car parking plot that comes with the hotel.

Our architect and planning consultant are drafting the layout drawings and design statement, for the planning application, and I have set up a meet and greet with the local ward councillors to informally take them through our plans for the building, which has sat almost derelict for the last three years.

It's a huge opportunity and one that we are very grateful to be given. It's going to require a big chunk of time, a massive dollop of graft, but the potential to be life changing. So please stay tuned and most of all, wish us luck!

CREATING VALUE THROUGH STRUCTURING AND PLANNING – TATIANA PREOBRAZHENSKAYA

"Someone's sitting in the shade today because someone planted a tree a long time ago" – Warren Buffett

Dear Readers, I hope you are finding this book enjoyable and gaining valuable insights into the world of commercial conversions. In this chapter I'll share some practical advice based on our experience with the 14 Unit Commercial Conversion in the heart of Leatherhead High Street in Surrey.

Just a few words about myself to give you an idea of where it all started.

Straight from University I joined the actuarial department of one of the Big four accounting firms in Moscow; four years later I moved to London in 2010 to pursue opportunities within Risk and Capital consulting team in Financial Solutions. The world of consulting is dynamic and stimulating and I loved every second of it until a certain point. As a young and hyper motivated team, we were thrown into multinational complex projects promising ground-breaking results to our clients within very constrained (often unachievable) timescales. What it meant for us, as a team, was absence of any work-life balance, endless business trips and a 24/7 work schedule all of which combined have created poor eating habits, disturbed sleep patterns, burn-outs and other quite predictable consequences. Naturally this path was not sustainable; life eventually caught up. The need for my personal time, space and freedom became more important than financial rewards and endless career prospects so we started looking for a new passion, where we could put ourselves first. The goal was to have control of our schedule and work-life balance, freedom to work with the people we chose and ultimately build a more efficient system of wealth creation for our family.

Project Description:

N25-29 Leatherhead High Street was our first commercial conversion project. We acquired it in January 2020 (just in time for COVID outbreak) via Allsop Residential Auction for £1.1m. We actually offered £50k higher prior to auction, but when the property did not sell, our slightly revised offer was accepted.

The existing building was a six-storey office building, with four storeys visible from Leatherhead High Street and another two storeys (lower ground and basement) which could only be seen from the Swan Centre, as the building was constructed on a steep slope. Prior approval was already granted for conversion of all storeys, except the ground floor, into 11 residential units. Ground floor unit was originally supposed to continue trading as class A (changed to class E under the current legislation).

The top three floors were already vacant possession and the basement was also vacated, although the official lease was still running for another two months. The lower ground and ground floors were occupied by a family-owned café. Although their lease was running until June 2026, they already owed over £100k in arrears so the plan was to ultimately ask them to vacate, once the conversion was largely complete.

Funding:

One of the greatest advantages of buying a commercial building is that you could use your SSAS (if you have one) to fund it. In this case, SSAS funding strategy substantially improved the economics of the project and reduced the need for equity to almost zero. Here is a brief structure chart:

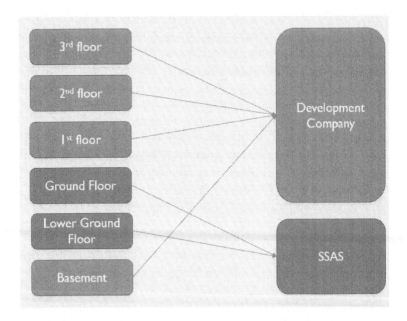

Out of £1.1m acquisition price, £350,000 was allocated to the Ground Floor Shop, which was not part of the conversion and could be held in our SSAS throughout the entire development. Even though the existing shop was struggling to pay their rent of £27,500 per annum, a few nearby shops have successfully secured tenants on similar terms, so the valuers accepted this rental figure without much challenge.

The Lower Ground Floor was eventually going to be converted into two flats so it could not be bought into the SSAS (as it would be a breach of HMRC Rules). However, it could be bought into an SPV and funded by SSAS via a loan back, as long as SSAS could secure a 1st charge. Another complication with the Lower Ground Floor was the fact that we still had to negotiate a Deed of Surrender so getting bank funding on it could have been challenging due to uncertainty around the timeline. SSAS on the other side was a perfect lender providing the flexibility needed.

As a result, out of £1.1m required, £425,000 was funded by our SSAS and the lender happily provided the rest secured on the freehold title with two floors 'sold off' on long leases.

If any readers of this book do not have their SSAS set up, I would highly recommend that they explore this option as it may help reduce the amount of equity and external debt required for any deal, increase profitability of the scheme (via lower cost of debt) and help secure some attractive returns for your pension scheme.

Value Adding Strategy:

When acquiring this project, we had a couple of ideas about how to further enhance the value of the project.

Step 1: Negotiate Surrender of the Lower Ground Floor Lease

Below are the originally approved plans for 11 units, however only nine of them could be implemented straight away. Naturally Step one was to negotiate Surrender with the existing Tenant. Given the level of arrears they had, the negotiation was quite easy and did not require any financial contribution from our side. This signed Deed of Surrender unlocked c. £110k of profits as it enabled us to convert the two additional units straight away (rather than wait for six years).

Step 2: Creating an extra unit by sub-dividing the basement space

As can be seen on the original plans presented above, the basement was quite spacious but only hosted one x two-bed unit due to the position of the access from the communal hallway. Creation of a second unit would usually require creating a long awkward corridor. From a desirability perspective, this was always going to be the greatest challenge. The future occupiers of the block would most likely be young students or working professionals trying to get on the property ladder and looking for the most affordable options. Estate agents

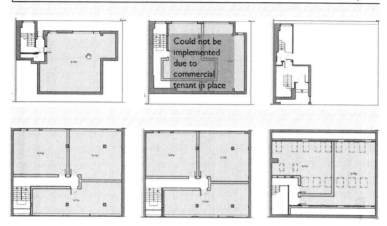

were doubtful regarding how much extra premium we would get for a second bedroom, in a basement location. All valuers pointed to the fact that price per sqm would drop so we were keen to find a way to split this space into two x one-bed units.

Having spoken to a fire consultant we noted the fact that the building had the rights to use the fire escape between N29 and N31, which was maintained by the Mole Valley Council. This enabled us to create a second entry point from the court-yard and sub-divide the basement unit into two x one-bed flats. We quickly re-submitted the prior approval application for 12 units, which was secured within eight weeks. These two x 33 sqm flats were ultimately sold for a combined value of £350,000 whilst the valuation for a 66 sqm unit was only £215,000, so this was a second rather valuable amendment.

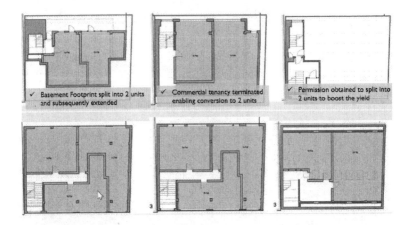

✓ Basement Footprint split into 2 units and subsequently extended
✓ Commercial tenancy terminated enabling conversion to 2 units
✓ Permission obtained to split into 2 units to boost the yield

Step 3: Conversion of Commercial Unit into Two Apartments

This was not part of our original strategy, however COVID hit us just as we were about to start the conversion in February/March 2020. With the current struggling tenant and massive scaffolds erected around the building, we knew we could not secure a reasonable rate. An ongoing wave of COVID 19 created additional uncertainly around the rental values and overall desirability for commercial space; we had to look for a plan B. We agreed with the current owner to continue operating without paying us any monthly rent, just as long as they continued to pay rather expensive Business Rates. They also agreed to share with us their management accounts, which we could use to demonstrate decreasing footfall and poor profitability. It was perfect timing to start marketing and build up the case for 'change of use' application with the council.

www.sustainomics.co.uk

Conveniently Class MA Permitted Development Rights were introduced in August 2021, just as we sold off the newly converted 12 units and completed 12 months of unsuccessful marketing the Ground Floor commercial unit. Our class MA application was approved on the first attempt and we converted the Ground Floor unit into two additional residential units as Phase 2 of this development so, ultimately, we converted the building into 14 apartments.

It is hard to assess how much value this third step actually added. If the originally assigned value of commercial unit of £350,000 was achievable at the time of exit, we may have never chosen to go ahead with the Phase 2 conversion. However, at the time, the demand for commercial units was very weak and whilst we were still getting interest, it was coming mostly from new inexperienced operators with rather weak covenants. It was quite obvious that if we continued with any of them, the rent would have to be reduced and the multiplier would fall, due to the poor covenant strength. As a result, as at August 2021, the value of the commercial unit had fallen to c. £250,000. Our secured Class MA conversion was still delivering a further £125k of profits as well as creating a certain exit strategy for our project.

Project Financials and Lessons Learnt:

Financial KPIs for this project are summarised below. The numbers include both phases, which ultimately took just over two years from acquisition to profits distribution.

If we were to compare the numbers above to the original appraisal, they would look quite different. As with any development project, things don't always go to plan and in this case COVID completely derailed our timeline. As described above we had to find alternative ways to add value to navigate through uncertainty and bring the economics back on track.

We learned a lot on the way and continue to apply the same principles on our current projects:

Gross Development Value	2,963,000
Purchase Price	1,100,000
Acquisition Costs	44,500
Conversion Costs Phase 1	734,500
Conversion Costs Phase 2	162,000
Professional Fees	41,500
Other Costs (Insurance, Warranties)	18,500
Sales Costs	35,556
Profit Before Interest & Tax	**826,444**
Finance Costs	114,000
Profit Before Tax	**712,444**

Watch your liquidity – planning and construction timescales can be very unpredictable. On the above site we were waiting for SES Water for seven months (to bring the 12 new connec-

tions) as they were not attending 'non-essential sites'. Our healthy liquidity position gave our lenders piece of mind.

Diversify – this is true of any investment and property is no exception. Diversifying across your projects is key as things WILL NOT go to plan.

Add value – for any project that we take, we have a value adding strategy (usually several). If you can't add value (and plan to implement the exact planning strategy already in place at time of acquisition), make sure you have plenty of contingency built into your appraisal.

Multiple exit strategies – having several exit strategies will always help you protect the value you created (especially to repay all interest-bearing debt). The timing may not always be perfect for sales; it is important to keep your options open and not force yourself to become a 'motivated seller'.

Thank you for reading my chapter and I hope you found some practical insights which you could implement in your projects. Best of luck in your commercial conversion journey.

OAK HOUSE, THE PROJECT THAT STARTED MY COMMERCIAL CONVERSION JOURNEY – LIAM RYAN

"If you don't find a way to make money while you sleep, you will work until you die" - Warren Buffet

It was the year 2016 which saw my first Commercial Conversion. It was also the year I joint ventured with my friends Mark Stokes and Nigel Greene and the year that I discovered the returns Commercial Conversions can make in a short period of time!

And it all started with a haircut! I know, sounds funny but it's true!

Our business partner, Nigel Greene, was walking into Colchester for a haircut one day, and, as a savvy property investor of many years who is always looking up at the local property market, rather than down at the pavement, spotted a sales board being fixed onto the side of a building.

Stopping to enquire, Nigel quickly learned that the building was coming on to the market for sale the next day.

A quick call to the commercial agent resulted in a returned call a few minutes later while he was sitting in the barber's chair!

Within two hours Nigel had secured a viewing of the property and by mid-day was touring the building.

The due diligence was quick to say the least that day, although he did know the area well, and after a quick conference call, we approved an offer and quickly submitted it during the afternoon.

While the first offer was not accepted, the revised offer later that afternoon was and that's where the Oak House development started! My first Join Venture with Mark and Nigel was cemented with what was to be a stunning Commercial Conversion project!

Shortly after securing the development, Mark and Nigel lost a private investor who had committed to invest but, due to personal circumstances, was now unable to. By coincidence I had secured a private investor but had just lost a deal. Mark and I belonged to the same Mastermind group and discussed this at length and quickly realised that we could joint venture and deliver this development together. A fantastic win:win resulting in over £500,000 of joint venture profit.

The current owner of the office building had the foresight to understand Permitted Development Rights, securing successful determination for eight two-bedroom apartments. Each of these apartments, however, were between 88 and 95m2, which is spacious for the target market!

Our strategy was to intensify the residential units by applying through Permitted Development Rights, for 16 x one-bedroom apartments.

This took one week to prepare and 45 days to be successfully determined, adding great value within weeks of securing the development.

So, that's how it all started. From Nigel's haircut to accepting the offer took just seven hours; it took a further few months forming a joint venture, raising the money and securing permitted development rights thus cementing life changing profits and 16 stunning homes for the local community.

Let me introduce you to Oak House in a bit more detail.

Oak House was an 8,500 sq. ft. (790m2) gross internal area office building, with a planning classification of B1a which is for office use.

It is located in a beautiful part of old Colchester (which is one of the oldest cities in the UK) in an area known as the Dutch Quarter, within 50m of the stunning Castle Park.

The building was constructed in the 1980s and was beginning to become tired; it was subdivided, by the previous owner, with plasterboard partitioning specifically to suit their business and how it had evolved over many years.

To give you an idea of the high-level programme of events for this development, we achieved the following timescales:

Nigel had a haircut!	Oct 16
Conditional Exchange	Dec 16
Intensified PD	April 17
Legal Completion	June 17
Soft Strip	June 17
Refurbishment starts	July 17
Help to Buy approved	Sept 17
Marketing phase 1	Nov 17
Marketing phase 2	Feb 18
Refurbishment completes	March 18
Apartments sold	June 18
Investor funds returned	July 18

The development was a great success, with phase one marketing resulting in 100% of reservations taken within TWO hours of release!

Financially the development was a great success too:

Gross Development Value	£2,683,000
Purchase Price	£900,000
Refurbishment	£850,000
Funding, professional fees etc	£350,000
Selling costs	£57,000
Net profit (pre-tax)	£526,000

During Construction Images:

Completed Images:

As part of the scheme, we secured confirmation of seven out of the sixteen apartments for Help To Buy support, which was available at the time.

Following the careful launch of phase one of the sales, we secured all seven sales reservations within hours of the launch. A 100% phase reservation confirmation!

We contacted the Help To Buy scheme and advised them of the clear demand in the area and the response to phase one sales release. They suggested we resubmit our application for the remaining nine apartments.

After only a few weeks, they responded and granted approval for 'Help To Buy' on the remaining nine apartments, thus giving 100% coverage across the entire development.

Persistence; the time-honoured quote of 'if at first you don't succeed, try, try and try again' springs to mind!

Success isn't left to chance and is the result of meticulous planning and attention to detail, anticipating every twist and turn possible and managing risk constantly.

Did everything always go right during the development? Well, despite its success we had challenges - after all, every development does! That is why we are so focused on risk management and have contingencies in many areas of our development appraisals.

So, wrapping up the story of Oak House – it's not just about my first Commercial Conversion success, but also about how something as ordinary as a haircut led to a pretty amazing project. Back in 2016, my friends Mark Stokes and Nigel Greene and I jumped into our first joint venture and all because we happened to notice a sales board going up on a building while heading for a haircut. Talk about being in the right place at the right time!

Within seven hours, from Nigel's haircut to us putting in an offer, we were on the road to creating Oak House – an iconic Commercial Conversion. The original plan for eight two-bedroom apartments got a boost when we decided to go for 16 one-bedroom units through Permitted Development Rights. The whole process, from prepping the proposal to getting the green light, took just over seven weeks.

Oak House stands tall as a testament to seizing opportunities and turning them into something awesome. From a spontaneous haircut to a thriving residential community, it's proof that in property development, a bit of innovation and a whole lot of determination can turn the unexpected into a success story.

PETALS AND PROGRESS – THE FLORAL TRANSFORMATION IN THE HEART OF THE LAKE DISTRICT – JONATHAN SHARPE

"If you do what is easy, life will be hard.
If you do what is hard, life will be easy"

In the pursuit of enhancing our family's quality of life, the journey into the realm of property investment transcended a mere financial venture. It evolved into a quest for purposeful transformation, a narrative that intertwines personal fulfilment and property development expertise. This chapter is a comprehensive chronicle of why the strategy of commercial conversions emerged as the guiding beacon on our path towards a brighter future.

Within the framework of property investment, each building harbours a unique narrative, a potential that patiently awaits its unveiling. It was here that commercial conversions, with their unparalleled blend of historical resonance and adaptability, resonated profoundly with our vision.

Beyond the bricks and mortar, we saw canvases for innovation, stages for revitalization and cornerstones for elevating not only physical spaces, but also the lives that intersect with them.

This chapter unfurls the intricacies of why commercial conversions became our chosen avenue.

The potential to breathe life back into forgotten edifices to our influential role in revitalizing entire communities, each facet reinforced our dedication to this dynamic strategy. The pages that follow will delve into the compelling reasons, strategic considerations and the transformative impact that commercial conversions can have on both property portfolios and, most significantly, the quality of life for our cherished family. Nestled in the heart of Ulverston, South Lakes, our development holds a special place in this vibrant town. Ulverston, a town steeped in history and brimming with character, provides the perfect canvas for this transformation. Positioned right in the bustling centre, this property promises not only modern, convenient living but also a respectful nod to its storied past.

Two years ago, the seed of this venture was planted when we stumbled upon this hidden gem on Rightmove. Our interest was piqued by its latent potential, but the journey was far from straightforward. Our initial offer was met with rejection, and it seemed that increased offers would also lead to closed doors. However, undeterred by the initial setback, we were fuelled by a steadfast belief in the untapped possibilities of this space. Through unwavering follow-ups with the local estate agent, we kept the conversation alive. It took time, patience, and an unwavering commitment, but eventually, our offer found the resonance it deserved.

Today, as we stand at the precipice of revitalizing this former computer repair shop, we are reminded that every great project begins with a seed of inspiration, nurtured by persistence and faith in its potential.

The journey into the acquisition and development of this site became a testament to the power of employing a diverse financial approach. By weaving together private investments, bridging loans, and personal funds, we crafted a complex, yet resilient financial framework. This not only facilitated the acquisition of the property, but also laid the foundation for its forthcoming transformation.

Throughout the development process, the main contractor emerged as an invaluable asset. Their professionalism and expertise significantly alleviated the stress typically associated with this stage. Of course, unforeseen challenges emerged along the way, but each one presented an opportunity for innovative problem-solving. These hurdles were navigated smoothly, ultimately contributing to the project's overall success.

The vision for this venture was nothing short of ambitious, but deeply purposeful, crafting a dynamic space comprising a vibrant hair salon and a well-appointed two-bedroom duplex apartment. This inspired concept led to the decision to allocate distinct titles for both the commercial and residential elements. The shop, a bustling hub of creativity, will be leased out under a fully repairing commercial agreement, ensuring its continued vitality. On the other hand, the duplex apartment, strategically located for optimal accessibility, will be operated as serviced accommodation. This dual-purpose approach not only complements the business model but also bolsters the cash flow, cementing the project's financial viability.

As a business, we find immense delight in the end product. The completed space stands as a testament to the pride and passion invested in every detail. The vibrant salon and thoughtfully designed apartment embody our unwavering commitment to creating spaces that inspire and enrich lives. We eagerly anticipate welcoming a thriving community within these walls, with each element reflecting our dedication to quality and excellence.

The property was acquired at £148,500, and we aspire to achieve a Gross Development Value (GDV) of £280,000. This ambitious target is substantiated by a hybrid valuation approach, a strategic decision that will enable our company to honour its commitments to investors and bridging lenders. Additionally, this approach allows us to reinvest our own funds into future projects, creating a sustainable cycle of growth and development. We eagerly anticipate not only realizing the potential of this venture, but also laying the groundwork for our next exciting endeavour.

Our exit strategy, carefully planned and executed, involves retaining the commercial space on the ground floor and dedicating the upper floors to serviced accommodation. This strategic move serves to maximize our cash flow, a vital component of our long-term financial sustainability. Moreover, the location's potential for significant capital growth further solidifies our decision to hold onto this property for the foreseeable future. It's a calculated move that aligns with our broader vision for sustained success in the property development arena.

Reflecting on this project, we've gleaned invaluable lessons. Our initial attempt to reduce development costs by taking on subcontractors ourselves, rather than relying on the main contractor's expertise, proved to be a costly misstep. It became evident that this approach didn't yield the intended savings and, instead, consumed valuable time and resources.

Effective cash flow management emerged as a critical learning point. Juggling multiple concurrent projects, alongside the intricacies of refinancing endeavours, underscored the importance of meticulous financial planning. This ensured seamless payments to our contractor, an essential element in maintaining project momentum and quality. These lessons have not only enriched our approach to this venture but will undoubtedly inform our strategies for future projects.

This experience has infused us with newfound confidence and knowledge. It has provided the stepping stones for us to tackle more substantial and profitable conversion projects. Armed with the lessons learned, we are poised to embark on even more ambitious ventures, fuelled by the belief that every project holds the potential for success and growth. The journey ahead promises to be exciting, and we're eager to take it on with unwavering determination and a wealth of experience behind us.

MY HUMBLE BEGINNING...
AND THE JOURNEY CONTINUES
– LAL DE SILVA

*"If you think you're too small to make a difference,
try sleeping with a mosquito"* — *Dalai Lama*

Hello, I'm Lal de Silva. I am from West London, where I live with my lovely wife and our two wonderful boys, Yohan and Dillan. My journey began in the beautiful land of Sri Lanka, a place that faced many challenges during the tumultuous '80s and '90s due to a brutal civil war. Growing up in such an environment, as a child, taught me resilience and strength.

My early career aspirations took me on quite a journey. Initially, I aimed to become an accountant and later a general manager in a luxury hotel. I started from the ground up in both fields. After a brief stint in the United States and the Caribbean, I arrived in the UK in the late '90s. I worked in the hospitality industry for a while before transitioning to a career in accounts. This journey eventually led to my role in Corporate Treasury, where I managed multi-million-pound portfolios by investing in money markets, executing currency hedging and more.

In my spare time, I dabbled in buy-to-let properties with limited knowledge of the subject. Surprisingly, I discovered that I could generate reasonable profits in property with relatively less time invested.

In 2008, during the heart of the recession, I encountered a crisis. I lost my job due to a restructuring, followed by a separation from my ex-wife. The job market was in turmoil and I couldn't secure a role that matched my previous salary. That's when I decided to venture into the world of property.

After gaining some necessary education, I embarked on a journey that began with starting a lettings business and then delving into HMOs (House in Multiple Occupation). I managed portfolios, sourced properties for other investors and leased some properties on a rent-to-rent basis. It wasn't long before I felt the urge to take the next step and explore property development.

I decided to focus on commercial conversions using permitted development rights. After evaluating numerous opportunities, I stumbled upon an old Methodist chapel, which had been converted into an office (formerly class O, now class E) in St Albans. This unique property was located in the heart of a residential neighbourhood, making it challenging for the agent to find a commercial buyer. Additionally, it sat within a conservation area and was locally listed. After crunching the numbers, I realised I could achieve a 20%+ Gross Development Value (GDV) by converting it into three apartments under PD rights.

Negotiations with the agent led to an offer at just £230 per square foot for purchase, while the residential square footage in the area commanded prices in the range of £500 to £550 per square foot.

I was determined to execute this project flawlessly, learning and earning along the way. I aimed to apply the same principles and strategies as I would with a larger development, which includes well-designed micro apartments with new build warranties, utilising the 'Help to Buy' scheme and building a strong team consisting of architects, Project managers and various consultants as well as securing development finance, as a first-time developer, to establish a track record.

However, as I navigated through this project, it presented numerous challenges. I encountered several rounds of permitted development applications, had to part ways with my first contractor under JCT terms and subsequently had to refinance the loan, due to time constraints. Covid lockdowns also meant the agreed sales could not progress. These challenges led to higher costs than initially budgeted, but I'm pleased to say that I managed to achieve my original GDV forecast and still exited the project with a profit.

Reflecting on this experience, I've learned several valuable lessons:

- Converting older buildings often requires more budget and contingency.

- As a developer, you are the driving force of your project, no matter how new you are to the field. Take control of your team and never be a passive participant.

- Aim for at least a 25% profit on GDV at the project's outset to provide a safety net when things go awry.

- Allow ample time from project inception to completion to handle unexpected delays.

- Gain a deep understanding of your cash flow when working with development finance.

- Develop a robust cash flow strategy for your project.

My journey didn't stop with the conversion of the chapel. I set new criteria/a wish list for my next venture—a permitted development project under Class MA with 25% or higher profit margins on GDV, ideally situated in West London, and also to collaborate with investors. After careful consideration,

I shortlisted several deals, and analysed potential schemes within the criteria with a preliminary planning consultant greenlight for permitted development. One such project was in the London Borough of Richmond.

The Richmond project featured a terraced shop with upper floors, located on the bustling Richmond Road. The shop, with 1,300 square feet of space, came with the freehold, while the upper floors were sold separately. The current owner had been running a convenience store for over 25 years but was looking to retire, given the drastic decline in sales after the opening of a Lidl store across the street.

I saw the potential to reduce the shop size to approximately 340 square feet and create a garden flat at the rear, all within the confines of Permitted Development under Class MA rights. While this seemed like an ideal situation in many aspects, several concerns loomed. The building was located in flood zone 3 albeit with a protective barrier, within the breach zone. It was also a conservation area. To make matters more challenging, Richmond council had recently approved an Article 4 direction that would prohibit the conversion of shops to residential use (Class C3) within 12 months, making future Class MA rights ineffective at the location.

When I first saw the property listed at £465,000 online, I couldn't make the numbers work, so I decided to park it. However, on a follow-up three months later, I learned that the property had gone under offer, but the deal fell through, and the price was reduced to £440,000. This time, I decided to pay a visit.

During my visit, I noticed that the agent's property description was rather lacking, and some vital information that could enhance the viability of the deal was omitted. I discovered a side return that wasn't mentioned and wasn't easily noticeable from inside the cluttered shop. Climbing a single-story

storage shed from the back alley, I realised that this addition could allow for roof lights, potentially leading to a larger flat with a second bedroom. That was a Eureka moment!

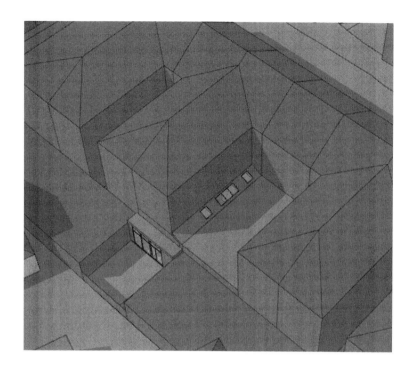

How we got light into the deep end of the flat

During this time, I received a call from Sean, whom I had met during my time in a commercial conversion mastermind group. He wanted to catch up over a coffee and as we caught up, we delved into my current property pipelines. At that moment, Richmond project was just one of several deals I had on my plate.

As we discussed the Richmond project's basic details, my colleague became more interested. Despite the deal being on the smaller side, he saw potential in funding it as a joint venture (JV). While I typically hesitated to enter JVs for smaller projects, it was one of my new criteria to work with JV partners, so I remained open to the possibility.

Our acquaintance with each other extended over a year, due to our participation in the same mastermind group, which gave me confidence in considering this venture. After further discussions and evaluations of the deal, we decided to proceed with an offer. The offer I put forth was £415,000 while the reduced asking was £440,000. To my pleasant surprise, it was swiftly accepted. This success came under the premise that our objective was to develop the property, not to secure commercial mortgages for re-establishing a convenience store.

This marked the beginning of our collaborative journey and set the stage for what lay ahead.

Under Class MA, the shop had to be vacant for three months at the time of application. As the shop was owner-occupied, vacant possession could only be granted after the purchase. To streamline the process and enhance the deal's figures, I requested that the three-month vacancy period be incorporated into the vendor's side of the agreement. This suggestion didn't sit well with the seller's agent, but after consulting with solicitors, we realised that as the freeholder, the seller had not yet issued Section 5 notices to the three leaseholders of the flats upstairs. This process takes a minimum of two months.

Consequently, we proposed that we exchange contracts, subject to no leaseholder exercising their Section 5 rights, and complete the transaction in ten weeks. Given that it was late

October 2021, the seller decided to shut down the business immediately after the exchange as his goal was to put his feet up by Christmas. This effectively gave us a nearly three-month vacancy period before our purchase.

Just before exchanging contracts, we engaged with the architect and planning consultant and collaborated on a game plan for executing the project in stages.

Stage 1 involved submitting a planning application to demolish the back storage unit to create garden space for a future flat, adding four roof windows in the side return for more light in the deep-end rooms, and installing a set of two-meter wide sliding doors at the back of the building to provide uninterrupted access to the garden from both the future master bedroom and living room.

Stage 2 involved the Class MA permitted development application incorporating the above-granted planning to convert the back part of the shop into a dwelling, reducing the size of the existing retail unit.

The project required meticulous planning and execution to gain class MA approval before Article 4, involving various consultants who produced reports within different timelines. These included a daylight-sunlight report, a noise test report, a flood consultant report with mitigation recommendations, a statement from a local commercial agent advocating for a smaller shop and a highway consultant's report.

By the time the successful approval was granted for the first planning application for windows and demolition, we advanced with obtaining consultant reports. Finally, the Class MA application was submitted in May 2022. With Article 4 scheduled to come into effect on July 31, we now only had this one shot to secure approval. A neighbouring council had recently rejected a Class MA application due to non-implementation of enabling planning toward permitted development. After discussing with our planning consultant, we decided to demonstrate our intent to convert the building by demolishing the storage unit, highlighting our commitment to the plan.

However, this very action backfired just two weeks before the decision date. The council asserted that the floor plans submitted with the Class MA application no longer matched the latest plans, due to the storage demolition. They suggested that we withdraw the application to avoid rejection on these grounds. Recognising that we were in a grey area, we decided to seek professional advice and engaged a planning barrister. The barrister's opinion was unequivocal - the council was making an incorrect and unlawful decision.

Upon submitting the barrister's opinion to the council, they promptly reversed their stance and chose to work with us. They requested a supplementary drawing showing the current floor plan and just two days after that, the Class MA was granted!

To move into the development phase, we needed to address discharging planning conditions, a Section 106 agreement with the council for a car-free arrangement, a waste management plan, a transport management plan and navigate five party wall notices. While we tackled these tasks, we tendered for builders with the assistance of an appointed project manager. We also decided to apply for a structural warranty for the flat to facilitate future financing. In January 2023, we brought the contractors on-site with an 18-week build program.

During the build phase, we encountered several challenges including the need for substantial additional structural work, utility complications that caused delays, and slower progress than anticipated by the contractors. In the end, the project took around 30 weeks - significantly longer than expected.

Amid these challenges, we encountered some positive surprises. Before the shop partitions were even completed, we engaged a local agent to gauge interest in the shop's rental. Initially, we anticipated £17,000 per annum for our newly created 340-square-foot shop. However, the agent suggested we market it at £22,000 to test the market. To our astonishment, we received three offers within a week. Following a bidding war, we secured a male groomer at £24,000 per annum on a 10-year guarantor-backed upward-only lease.

Additionally, the flat was finally marketed in September and has recently gone under offer.

Let's compare the project's financials from the start to its current status:

January 2022 | November 2023 Costs:

Purchase: £415,000 | - Purchase: £415,000

Stamp Duty: £10,250 | - Stamp Duty: £10,250

Conversion: £106,050 | - Conversion: £170,000

Professional: £25,000 | - Professional: £57,000

Finance: £45,000 | - Finance: £76,000

Total: £601,300 | - Total: £728,250

GDV:

Shop: £283,333 (£17,000 @ 6%) | - Shop: £343,000 (£24,000 @ 7%)

Flat: £575,000 | - Flat: £625,000

Total: £858,333 | - Total: £968,000

Profits:

£257,033 | £239,750

On GDV: 30% | - On GDV: 24%

On Costs: 42% | - On Costs: 32%

This project surely pushed me further in my property development journey, allowing me to learn more and adapt quickly. I had to make executive decisions in real time, such as standing my ground with building control regarding fire safety measures, which led to substantial savings. I also negotiated to reduce exorbitant fees for electricity connections, showcasing the importance of thorough research and expert advice.

Moreover, working with my JV partner, Sean Harrison has been a valuable experience. I'd also like to acknowledge David Kemp, who provided excellent guidance as our planning consultant, and Mark Stokes, a mentor and a true friend who invited me to contribute to this remarkable book.

Property development has not only opened doors to me as an entrepreneur but also led to my personal development, enabling me to connect with exceptional individuals in this close-knit community. I'm truly humbled to be a part of this journey so far and hope to meet all of you and share our experiences in the near future.

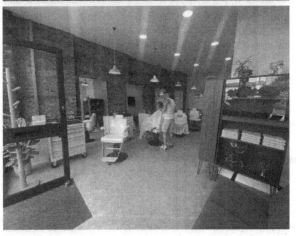

LOOK FOR OPPORTUNITY WHERE OTHERS AREN'T – WILLIAM STOKES

"Everything around you that you call 'life' was made up by people who were no smarter than you" – Steve Jobs

Starting the chapter of any book is hard enough, let alone the only chapter I'm actually having to write, but here goes.

For those who don't already know me, my name's William. I've spent the last nine years within the property sector and currently run a commercial workspace developer and operator called Co-Space. We focus on creating design-led workspace for growing SME's in tier 2 locations.

What is a 'commercial workspace developer and operator' I hear you say? It's basically a fancy way of saying we develop office space and then work really hard to tenant that space for our own portfolio. Think half commercial developer and half WeWork, just without the Chapter 11.

Before co-founding Co-Space in 2018, I worked closely with Mark and the team at Equa buying and developing commercial to residential schemes in the home counties. No doubt his chapter will bring you up to speed.

In what feels like a lifetime ago, I started my career as an engineer but quickly moved from design to project management. Back then I would never have thought I'd end up here, trying to impart the knowledge I've learnt over a nearly 15-year career, but as I look back the steps all align in one way or another.

To date Co-Space has developed three projects - Reading, Stevenage and Milton Keynes. At the time of writing this chapter we've just completed on our fourth project, although sadly I can't say much more beyond that, at this stage. This next project will be our best one yet I think - maybe I'll be writing about project number four in some other book down the line, who knows, but for now this chapter is going to focus on arguably one of my favourite projects to date - Co-Space Stevenage.

Stevenage is perhaps famous for one of two reasons. The first for all you Formula 1 fans out there, Stevenage is the birth-place of eight-time world champion and all round GOAT Lewis Hamilton. Don't worry, I know it's seven, but we all know 2021 should have been number eight right?! Secondly, following the celebrity theme, it's also the birthplace of Ed Westwick, AKA Chuck Bass - XOXO for those who know. Beyond that, being the last stop for anyone heading into London from the North, is about the only other thing that used to be going for the place. That is at least until the local council pushed central government for a total regeneration of the area.

If you're sceptical don't worry, I was too at first. Walking into the town square back in 2019 I wondered what we were getting ourselves into. We knew the area was undergoing a widespread regeneration, but we didn't bank on rocking up on day one - I mean the work had literally only just started. The next person I met was the head of regen, a guy called Nick. Over the course of the next four hours, a guy who when I say 'bleeds' Stevenage, like Gary Neville bleeds Manchester, is not an understatement, truly convinced myself and my business partner, Ali, that Stevenage was in fact the right place for Co-Space to be.

Reading, our first site, is 25 minutes from London. The market is hot and perfect for working or commuting into the city; Stevenage, by contrast, is 19 minutes from London and yet seemed more remote than when I lived back in Lincoln. Lincoln is great, but it's not a place you pass through - you have to actually want to go there. Stevenage was a pass-through

www.sustainomics.co.uk

location, the first in fact for anyone leaving London, and yet this wasn't being reflected.

Looking back now, going to Stevenage and undertaking project number two there was by far one of the best decisions we've ever made. We wanted the site to be a success but back in 2019 we just hoped the rest of the region would catch up and soon. Thankfully, after spending nearly a year on site, and launching in September 2021, Stevenage has truly become a great place to work and live, even if the rest of the UK hasn't caught on yet!

So, by now I'm sure you're wondering what makes this development in Stevenage so special? Let me tell you more. Firstly, let me give you the overall site specifics, the stuff that hopefully gives some wider context to the real size and scope of the scheme. The site is 16,080 sq/ft GIA. For those in the resi side of development, that's typically around 32-36 apartments. We occupy two floors above the prominent high street retail, as well as a three-storey atrium we created right in the middle of the high street connecting the first and second floor to the ground floor entrance. Prior to us coming into the scheme, the west wing was home to McDonald's with some rather tired office space above. The east wing of the scheme was retail storage and generally disused space. The site was a wreck by the time we stepped in and needed a big vision to really bring the scheme and Stevenage into the 21st century.

Firstly, let me tell you, nothing can truly prepare you for how long you're going to spend in legals. Whilst lawyers are incredibly smart, much smarter than myself, they don't half sometimes get caught up in trivial points. We spent a whopping 15 months engaged. Just under three months agreeing HoT's and then exchange, and then a further 12 months before we could actually get the keys and get started. Finally, in December of 2020 we managed to drive it over the line. Or should I say Ali did - he's far better at the more detailed stuff; I just like to run off and get things built.

Prior to completion we had already created the stage 3/4 design pack; we do this all in-house to ensure we know exactly what we're getting priced. Typically, it takes more time up front and it's worth noting, pre-completion, it is a risk and sits within your sunk capital funds, but over the full cycle of the project, having a detailed design up front will give a clearer picture on costs and save time during the build phase. There's no push back saying something wasn't specified, it's all there in black and white. Thankfully we have some of the best designers in the world. Shout out Tiff at Waistcoat and Badger.

As part of the completion requirements, we worked closely with the council, overall owner of the scheme, to ensure the prep works we required were undertaken. For instance, the ground outside the front of the soon to be atrium ran at a slope. We pushed the council to undertake the levelling off works as one of the-pre commencement conditions. We didn't want to be dealing with highways on that one - no thank you!

Finally, after what felt like the longest year of our lives, we were able to get started on site towards the end of 2020. As I'm sure many of you were also affected by the Covid-19 pandemic, we thankfully were able to remain active throughout, apart from the March '20 - June '20 full lockdown. The design team were also able to ensure we had everything ready to go, once we were able to crack on.

As I'm sure many of you know, the vision for the project really starts on that first site visit. As developers we have to see what a building truly can be and look, past the current condition. Whilst the end product may look stunning, those early days are anything but. If I don't come away from a visit really excited about the possibility of transforming any kind of space, I'm pretty quick to realise it's not one for us.

I have a really simple process to appraise any opportunity we look at. Whilst looking at a floorplan or brochure is great, nothing really immerses you like walking around the site and walking around the local area. Almost always we like to visit a site if it's a) within our target area and location, ie close to transport links and so on, and b) fits within our criteria of 15,000-30,000 sq/ft, ground floor presence and ideally roof space or parking. From there we'll get a feel for whether we think a space will truly work for us. Step two is pretty simple - over the last three years we've really refined our deal anal-yser. In fact, it plugs directly into our operating cash flow fore-cast. I simply put in the sq/ft, a few assumptions on the return profile, typically all sq/ft driven, and pretty quickly I can see what the back end looks like. We have a strict 20% EBITDA return on our operating side, with a minimum return of £200k EBITDA pa, and an IRR of 15% pa on the development side. If we can achieve those two metrics, the site works both finan-cially and gives us the permission to get really excited.

For context, EBITDA is the business earnings before interest such as loans, tax, amortisation and depreciation. Most busi-

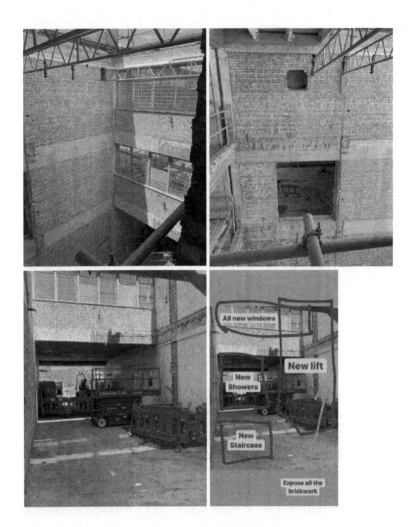

nesses get valued in some way linked to EBITDA. IRR is your internal rate of return - in short, the higher the IRR, the better the overall return. Back to property.

Your strategy might be different; for instance a good friend of mine targets £250k return after all costs on his schemes. Doesn't matter if its £1.4m or £3m GDV, as long as he can

make £250k - he's happy! Admittedly, the longest scheme he'll look at is 18 months. £250k return gets less and less exciting the longer a scheme goes on. Anything below 10% IRR is a no go in my eyes.

Back to Stevenage. Let me give you the overview of what we did, and then dive into some of the key takeaways. So, as you know, after what felt like an age of legals and design work we were finally able to get started. The first thing we did was replace the roof and replace all the windows. Remember when I said the site was made up of retail storage and tired office space? Well, I left one bit out. Right in the heart of the scheme, connecting the east wing to the west wing, was a three-storey Ladbrokes. That's right, one of those betting shops you've likely walked past and wondered if its either open or who on earth goes in there! This was, thankfully, part of our scheme and thankfully VP (vacant possession) when we took over. When buying a site, if your plan is to evict the tenants because you require the space on day one, the best way is to insist the site is vacant possession upon legal completion. Leave the current owner responsible. So, thankfully it was vacant because we took a literal bulldozer through the centre of the building. In doing so we revealed some of the original brickwork and structural beams. Our plan on day one was to create a nice clean entrance, but upon uncovering all the original brick work we just knew it had to remain exposed. Check it out below.

On the opposite side of the scheme there was an old redundant staircase connecting the first and the second floor, right where we wanted a walkway. You guessed it - that had to go too! We carefully, and purposely, created a scar in the wall where the staircase had once been to create a feature timeline of the overall scheme. Remember when I said its in the heart of Stevenage? I wasn't lying - this site was the first site build in what became Stevenage new town. Talk about history.

Overall, we spend £2.03m on the scheme, broken into two packages. The first was the major shell and core works. Things like replacing the windows, the roof, and pouring the lift shaft. That package came to just over £500k. The major CAT A & B works came to £1.53m at final account. The budget was

£1.57m - how's that for 'on budget'. The main reason for this is because as I said before, we designed it all up front, we knew exactly what we were getting. It also helps we didn't uncover anything too onerous too.

In everything we do, we look at ways to utilise both the fabric of the building and as many of the existing features as possible. Being able to mix the old and the new really creates a unique modernisation of what would typically be knocked down and built again.

For us, product is key. We spend money where others wouldn't - from 12.8mm glass to create better acoustics, to installing individually controlled HVAC in every office. We've set out to create the kind of office space Stevenage, and every other Co-Space location, truly deserves.

Developing assets for our own portfolio means we can keep a very close eye on what the end product should really be. If we try to shave costs or cut corners, it will inevitably bite us in the operating side. We ensure everyone across the business is aligned with exactly what we're creating - and more importantly where.

I'm going to finish with a few pictures of the space, both before and after, but hopefully I've been able to showcase why looking in markets others aren't, might just be a good idea and why you have to focus on the end goal from day one, with any scheme. Always ask yourself - is my target market going to want this? If not, adjust.

A JOURNEY BEGINS
– JAKE SUTHERS

"Creative problem-solving is rewarding:
Finding innovative solutions made this project possible"

In the bustling streets of Dubai, where we both worked full-time jobs - me as a Quantity Surveyor and my soon-to-be wife in Financial Services - my journey of personal growth took shape. It all started with a chance encounter with Robert Kiyosaki's 'Rich Dad Poor Dad' while I was reluctantly wandering through a garden centre in scorching 40-degree heat. This discovery completely transformed my outlook on life and within just a few weeks, I underwent a significant shift.

My time in the UAE was fortunate, with a secure job at a prominent firm, where I worked on extensive projects. During this period, I began to see a connection between my daily work and the potential for residential development, albeit on a smaller scale.

After five years in Dubai, I returned to the UK in February 2020, just as the COVID-19 lockdowns began. My wife was pregnant with our first child, and our third residential project, originally intended for sale, was put on hold. I brought my job with me from Dubai, but the uncertainty of the times made me explore other income options. Could I expand my property development efforts? I scoured property listings and worked with local estate agents to find off-market or below-market-value opportunities. My skills as a Quantity Surveyor and my knack for deal analysis proved valuable as I brokered deals and supervised renovations for extra income. However, this period posed challenges for everyone, with mortgages becoming harder to secure, skilled tradesmen in short supply and good deals increasingly rare. I dedicated all my free time to this side hustle.

As I became more involved in property development circles, I noticed a shortage of skilled Quantity Surveyors. Meanwhile, my employer wanted me to return to their Manchester offices, which would mean long hours, separation from my new-born son and growing dissatisfaction. I decided to take a bold step and establish my own Quantity Surveying firm. This move allowed me to balance my day job and nurture my true passion – development. This pivotal decision was made in 2021, and as we fast-forward to 2023, the future looks promising.

Enter the Dog and Partridge, a development that took two challenging years to reach the planning approval stage. As I scoured agency websites for opportunities, this former pub kept coming up. It had been on the market since the start of the pandemic as the previous owners, who had run it as a family business for nearly a century, reluctantly decided to sell. The property, nestled in the Ribble Valley, was located within an Area of Outstanding Natural Beauty, making it attractive to hikers and those seeking rural tranquillity. The potential for development was clear.

However, the numbers didn't add up. The purchase price was too high and estate agents weren't very helpful. I decided to take a different approach - I managed to get the vendor's phone number and started a conversation. Little did I know that this initial contact would lead to a two-year relationship marked by extensive conversations over tea and scones, resulting in a mutually beneficial outcome.

Early in our discussions, it became clear that a traditional sale and purchase agreement wouldn't work. I wanted to help them to carry out the development, but the initial asking price was unrealistic, especially given the property market's inflation. There was more at stake than just a transaction; this place held deep sentimental value as a nurturing environment for family, with the comforting presence of relatives. I considered various options – adjusting the purchase price, extending the completion timeline, or even selling my own home and moving into the pub's flat to make it work. None of these options felt entirely right. Our discussions went back and forth for months.

It took six months of persistent negotiation to reach an agreement that finally made sense to both parties.

In October 2023, after countless setbacks, discussions with the local council, objections from concerned neighbours and endless reports and design changes, we finally obtained planning permission. We were given the green light to transform the former pub into six one and two-bedroom apartments, along with a two-bedroom bungalow and a workshop for the current owners. Additionally, three two-bedroom holiday accommodations would be built at the rear. The journey to this point had been tough.

In November 2023, we began our project and we're on track to finish by the end of 2024. Our initial work includes renovating the vendor's bungalow and preparing the ground for holiday accommodations. My business partner, who's the contractor for this project, is fully committed to ensuring a 12-month turnaround with his team.

Our exit plan is as follows - the vendors will keep the bungalow as their home. The six remaining flats in the existing building will be sold to private residents, while our management company will handle the holiday lets. We'll refinance everything after completing the project, to repay our lenders.

From the moment I read that life-changing book in Dubai in 2016 to now, it feels like I've achieved the impossible. I've learned through taking action and making bold choices, especially when I left corporate life for entrepreneurship. These decisions have not only impacted my life, but also the vendors and their families.

Looking back, the main lessons from this venture are:

1. Creative problem-solving is rewarding - Finding innovative solutions made this project possible. Understanding the motivations of the vendors led to a unique opportunity.

2. Patience is vital - Dealing with setbacks and diverse interests requires empathy and patience, leading to mutually beneficial solutions, even if it takes time.

3. Adequate seed capital is essential - Don't rush into a venture without being financially prepared. Planning can involve substantial expenses.

4. Fairness with investment partners is key - Sharing risks and rewards equitably is not only fair, but also wise.

5. Knowing the bank's allowable fees is crucial.

I'm carrying these lessons with me into my next development - an existing office and retail building in the heart of Preston, my hometown and where I live now. This purchase has been in progress alongside the Dog and Partridge project – you know what they say, "You wait for one bus, and two come along at once?" Well, I'm catching that bus!

EXISTING BUILDING:

ARIEL VIEW OF EXISTING BUILDING AND LAND

AONB VIEW

RENDERING OF NEW DEVELOPMENT

PROPOSED LAYOUT OF FLATS AND BUNGALOW IN EXISTING BUILDING

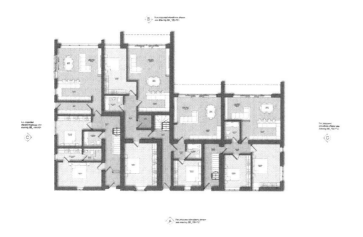

PROPOSED VIEW OF HOLIDAY LETS AND REAR OF EXISTING BUILDING DEVELOPMENT

ARIEL VIEW OF REDEVELOPMENT

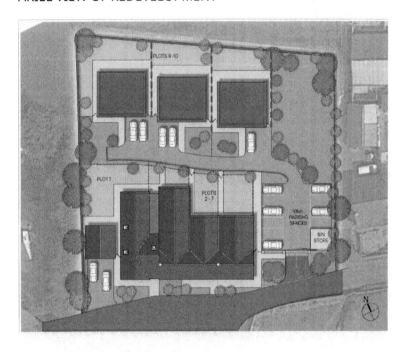

PROPOSED DESIGN OF HOLIDAY LETS

ACCOMMODATION SCHEDULE

Pub Conversion

No	Floor	Unit	Amenity	Parking	Area (m2)	Area (ft2)
1	Ground	2 Bed Flat	Garden Area	1 parking space	109	1,173
2	Ground	1 Bed Flat	Garden Area	1 parking space	56	603
3	Ground	2 Bed Flat	Garden Area	1 parking space	85	915
4	First	2 Bed Flat	Balcony	1 parking space	88	947
5	First	1 Bed Flat	Balcony	1 parking space	65	700
6	First	2 Bed Flat	Balcony	1 parking space	85	915

New Build Bungalows

No	Floor	Unit	Amenity	Parking	Area (m2)	Area (ft2)
1	Ground	2-Bed Bungalow	Garden area	1 parking	86	926
2	Ground	2-Bed Bungalow	Garden area	1 parking	86	926
3	Ground	2-Bed Bungalow	Garden area	1 parking	86	926

FINANCIALS:

			LOW	MID-POINT	HIGH
0	Gross Development Value		£2,844,037	£3,097,019	£3,350,000
		Total	£2,844,037	£3,097,019	£3,350,000

COSTS

			LOW	MID-POINT	HIGH
1	Land Purchase		£350,000	£350,000	£350,000
2	Build Costs		£1,514,000	£1,514,000	£1,514,000
3	Contingency (Build only)		£151,400	£151,400	£151,400
4	Conveyancing Costs		£33,000	£33,000	£33,000
5	Funding Costs		£20,275	£20,275	£20,275
6	Reports & Surveys		£11,398	£11,398	£11,398
7	SPV Set-up and running costs		£3,250	£3,250	£3,250
8	Project Management and Design		£83,308	£83,308	£83,308
9	Planning Fees and Costs		£6,038	£6,038	£6,038
10	Local authority Costs and Charges		£900	£900	£900
11	Utility Connections		£18,000	£18,000	£18,000
12	Marketing & Exit Costs		£14,400	£14,400	£14,400
13	Other Reports, Fees and Costs		£35,973	£35,973	£35,973
14	Selling Costs		£21,750	£21,750	£21,750
15	Cost of Funds		£148,809	£148,809	£148,809
		Total	£2,412,501	£2,412,501	£2,412,501

PROFIT (EBITDA)

		LOW	MID-POINT	HIGH
16	Profit (EBITDA)	431,536	£684,517	£937,499
17	PoCost%	17.89%	28.37%	38.86%
18	PoGDV%	15.17%	22.10%	27.99%

Structure:

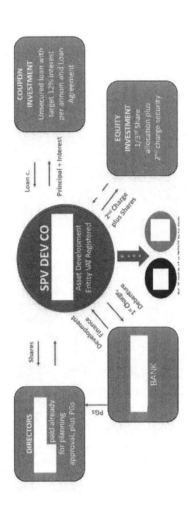

ABOUT MARK STOKES

With over 30 years' experience at C-suite level in international businesses, Mark has a strong passion for creating shared value and inspiring others to achieve assured outcomes.

In 2024, Mark celebrates 25 years of mentoring business leaders and management teams, entrepreneurs and individuals looking to live their best life.

Mark has delivered almost four million sq ft of commercial real estate conversions across 33 countries and, in recent years, over £90m GDV of commercial to residential conversions.

His passion for guiding and supporting talent to out-perform consistently and deliver outstanding organisational performance has led him to invest in, and acquire, numerous businesses for which he remains passionate about through his business www.sustainomics.co.uk.

Mark has founded and operated many national and international businesses across multiple sectors including construction, infrastructure, technology, telecommunications, professional services, education and real estate. He has also pioneered ESG principles since 2007, delivering accountable social impact investments to our communities.

For over 20 years, Mark has been a business leader, non-executive director and corporate trouble shooter; his expertise spans business acquisitions, private investor relations, structuring, strategy and leadership at all stages in businesses ranging from start-up, growth, turn-around, sale, mergers and acquisitions.

His passion for creating shared value has led Mark to become nationally recognised as an author, publishing six highly acclaimed and best-selling books available on Amazon and is a highly sought after business consultant, investor and non-executive director.

To contact Mark directly regarding mentorship and consultancy please drop him a line at mark@sustainomics.co.uk

OTHER BOOKS FROM MARK STOKES

Property & SSAS Secrets

Imagine if you had all the funds you need to create a property portfolio that will enable your family's financial independence. Well, this book will show you how that is possible with a SSAS (Small Self-Administered Scheme) pension.

SSAS Pensions: Creating extraordinary levels of compounding wealth

If you are serious and passionate about having flexibility in your investment strategy, leaving a legacy and planning for the long-term - then this book is a must read.

Commercial to Residential Conversions: The essential manual for property developers

This essential manual by business and development expert, Mark Stokes, is based on his three decades experiencing global corporate life.

Advice to Your Younger Self

If you could wind the clock back, what advice would you give your younger self? Imagine how life might be different if you knew then, what you know now.

SSAS Superstars: How 10 Entrepreneurs Unlocked Their Pensions, Without Waiting to Retire

SSAS Superstars shines a light on ten entrepreneurs who show you how to grow your personal wealth, reaching financial security and beyond.

www.sustainomics.co.uk

Notes

Notes

Notes

Notes

Printed in Great Britain
by Amazon